P9-DMP-562

Eyewitness
SPACE
EXPLORATION

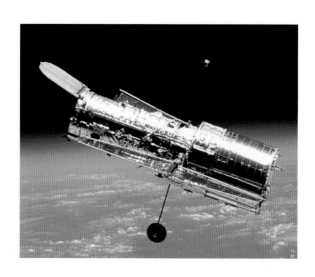

Hubble Space
Telescope

Potential damage
of space dust on
shuttle window

Satellite material

Japanese space agency
(NASDA) lapel badge

Toys taken into space

Spacesuit
designed for
use on the Moon

Patch worn by
first Mongolian
in space

Giotto space
probe

McDonald's toys
encouraging youth
interest in space

Residue
from solid
rocket boosters

Vase commemorating Polish
and Soviet space flight

Eyewitness
SPACE
EXPLORATION

In-flight space clothes
worn on Mir

Written by
CAROLE STOTT

Photographed by
STEVE GORTON

Mir space station

Badge of Soviet
shuttle, Buran

Dorling Kindersley

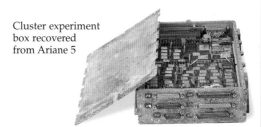

Cluster experiment
box recovered
from Ariane 5

Astronaut training in
harness simulating
weightlessness

LONDON, NEW YORK, MUNICH,
MELBOURNE, and DELHI

Project editor Kitty Blount
Art editor Kati Poynor
Editor Julie Ferris
Managing editor Linda Martin
Managing art editor Julia Harris
Production Lisa Moss
Picture research Mo Sheerin
DTP Designer Nicky Studdart

PAPERBACK EDITION
Managing editor Andrew Macintyre
Managing art editor Jane Thomas
Editor Francesca Baines
Art editor Catherine Goldsmith
Production Jenny Jacoby
Picture research Sarah Pownall
DTP designer Siu Yin Ho
6 8 10 9 7

This Eyewitness ® Guide has been conceived by
Dorling Kindersley Limited and Editions Gallimard

Hardback edition first published in Great Britain in 1997.
This edition published in Great Britain in 2002
by Dorling Kindersley Limited,
80 Strand, London WC2R ORL

Copyright © 1997, © 2002, Dorling Kindersley Limited, London
A Pearson Company

All rights reserved. No part of this publication may be
reproduced, stored in a retrieval system, or transmitted
in any form or by any means, electronic, mechanical,
photocopying, recording or otherwise, without the
prior written permission of the copyright owner.

A CIP catalogue record for this book is
available from the British Library.

ISBN 0 7513 4750 7

Colour reproduction by
Colourscan, Singapore
Printed in Hong Kong by Toppan

See our complete catalogue at

www.dk.com

Telstar – transmitted first
live satellite television

Space food:
dehydrated fruit

Ariane 5 rocket

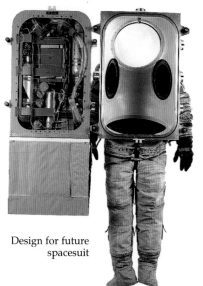
Design for future
spacesuit

Patch worn by Sigmund Jahn, the first
astronaut of the German Democratic Republic

Patch celebrating the first Indian
astronaut, Rakesh Sharma

Contents

Dreams of space

WINGED FLIGHT
In Greek mythology, Daedalus made a pair of wings for himself and his son Icarus, in order to escape from a labyrinth. The wings were attached to their bodies with wax. But impetuous Icarus flew too close to the Sun, the wax melted, and he fell to Earth.

Humans have always looked into the sky and wondered about what lies beyond the Earth. For many, their curiosity stops there. Others dream of journeying into space, exploring the Moon, landing on Mars, or travelling to the stars. The dream of space travel and exploration turned to reality in the 20th century. The first practical steps were taken at the start of the century as rockets were developed to blast away from Earth. In 1961, the first person reached space. By the end of the century, thousands of spacecraft and hundreds of space travellers had been launched into space. For many, the dream continues. A new generation of space travellers wants to go further, stay longer, and learn more about space.

FACT MEETS FICTION
As humans learnt more about their surroundings in space, the stories of space travel became more realistic. In the late 19th century, the French author Jules Verne wrote stories using fact as well as science fiction. His characters journeyed to the Moon in a shell fired by a giant cannon.

GOOSE TRAVEL
The Moon, Earth's closest neighbour, looms large in the sky. Light and dark areas on its surface are clearly visible. Its apparent proximity made it the object of many dream journeys into space. In a 17th century story, wild geese took 11 days to carry a man to the Moon.

SKY WATCHING
Our present knowledge of space is partly built on information learnt by ancient civilizations. Thousands of years ago, basic distances were established and the regular movements of the Sun, Moon, and planets were used for timekeeping and to understand how Earth fitted into the Universe.

MUSIC OF SPACE
Space and its contents – the Moon, planets, and stars – have inspired story writers, poets, and musicians. In 1916, Gustav Holst, a Swedish composer, completed an orchestral suite called "The Planets". As the space race was gathering momentum, the American singer Frank Sinatra (left) was performing love ballads including "Fly Me to the Moon". And the Moon has often been depicted as a magical land in rhymes and stories for children.

TELESCOPE POWER
Until the 17th century, people believed that the Sun, Moon, planets, and stars all revolved around Earth. Observations made by Galileo Galilei, an Italian, through the newly invented telescope showed that space was much bigger and contained more than had been thought, and helped show that humankind was not at its centre.

SPACE MONEY
This Moscow statue of a rocket being launched is a mark of the national feeling in Russia for their astronauts and space exploration. In the 1940s and 1950s, research into space travel had been developed by national governments, and began to receive serious financial backing. Policies for space travel and exploration, and strategies for using space were established.

SPACE POP

Space arrived in the high street in the 1960s and 1970s when fashion and pop music showed the influence of the space age. David Bowie (right) took on the persona of spaceman Ziggy Stardust, and his songs "Space Oddity" and "Is There Life on Mars?" echoed the concerns of the space scientists.

Exploring the Moon would soon become a reality

COMIC CAPERS

The dream of space was at its wildest in the comics of the 1930s through to the 1950s. Authors and artists let their imaginations run riot. Aliens were featured regularly, from encounters in space to landings on Everest. But many other stories were not so far-fetched, and only heralded space ventures that were to become reality within decades.

CLUB TOGETHER

Individuals dreaming of space travel club together to form societies. The first was established in Germany in 1927, followed by America and Britain. A leading figure in the British society was Arthur C. Clarke, whose ideas helped to influence space research. His articles and books deal with science fiction as well as science fact. He foresaw the use of satellites for communicating globally and showed us the space future in his books and articles and also in the innovative film *2001: A Space Odyssey*.

Earth seen from the Moon

Cratered lunar surface

Astronaut holding American flag

20TH CENTURY ICON

In 1986, medieval figures that had adorned the roof of Britain's York Minster Cathedral were destroyed in a fire. They were replaced by this potent symbol of the 20th century – humankind conquering space. For hundreds of years to come, worshipping Christians will gaze up at this icon of our times.

SPACE HERO AND HEROINE

Today's children were born into the space age and know that space exploration is a reality. They understand how a satellite works, they know what space is like and they look forward to exploring it. Even young children's toy hero Action Man (right) and heroine Barbie (above) have apparently both been to space!

What is space?

SURROUNDING EARTH IS A BLANKET OF AIR, its atmosphere. It both provides the oxygen we need to stay alive, and protects us from the heat of the Sun in the day, and from the cold, sunless night. Away from Earth's surface, the air thins and its composition and temperature change. It becomes increasingly difficult for a person to survive. The changes continue as the altitude increases and space approaches. The transition from Earth's atmosphere to space is gradual; there is no obvious barrier to cross. Above say 1,000 km (621 miles) from Earth is space, but many conditions associated with space are experienced within a few hundred kilometres of Earth, where satellites and astronauts work.

DUSTY DANGER
Space is virtually empty, but anything sent into it has to be shielded against natural or man-made dust specks, which move through space faster than bullets. This test shows how a tiny piece of nylon, travelling at the speed of a space dust speck, can damage metal.

Nylon missile

Lead with large hole

Stainless steel with smaller hole

Astronaut, inside a craft in a constant state of fall, feels weightless

WEIGHTLESSNESS
Astronauts, like these in the space shuttle, can neither see nor feel gravity working on them. But it is there. Their spacecraft is constantly being pulled by Earth's gravity. It resists the pull and stays in orbit by attempting to travel away from its orbit.

Rigil Kentaurus, which is the third brightest star in the night sky

The plane of the Milky Way Galaxy

ROLLER COASTER
As a car goes over a hump in the road, the passengers' stomachs fall slightly after their body frames. They momentarily experience weightlessness. A roller coaster ride has a more dramatic effect, and the feeling can last for a few seconds. Modified aircraft give astronauts the chance to train in weightlessness for about 25 seconds.

At the top of the steepest rides, it is claimed, passengers are weightless for up to six seconds

LOOKING INTO SPACE

When we look at the night sky, we can see tens of thousands of stars, which, like the Sun, our own star, belong to the Milky Way Galaxy, partly shown here. Beyond are about 100, billion, billion stars in other galaxies, which, along with trillions of kilometres of virtually empty space, make up the rest of the Universe. We have only explored space within the Solar System, made up of the Sun and the planets that orbit around it.

HUMANS IN SPACE

Most astronauts, like these ones, have travelled into space close to Earth, where they use the planet's gravity to orbit around it. Only 26 have travelled further, to the Moon. Wherever humans go in space, they need to take their own atmosphere and protection against the new environment.

Suits protect astronauts from temperatures ranging from 121°C (250°F) to -101°C (-150°F)

Rock from Mars fell to Earth about 13,000 years ago

Voyager spacecraft is prepared for launch in 1977

DOWN TO EARTH

Scientists get the chance to study space material by sending robotic craft, or astronauts, to investigate it on site, or bring it back to Earth. They also study chunks of it that have found their own way here. Every year, over 3,000 bits of space rock fall to Earth. Most go in the sea, but a handful are collected.

MESSAGE FROM EARTH

It is believed that one in every twenty-five stars has planets. The Sun has nine and since 1995 more have been discovered orbiting other stars. Of these, Earth is the only planet known to have life. However, some spacecraft, such as Voyager, carry messages in case intelligent life does exist elsewhere.

Disc with message

HIGH ALTITUDE EXPLORERS

There is no need to leave Earth to experience a change in altitude and a consequent change in Earth's atmosphere. Mountaineers know that the air gets thinner the higher they climb. At around 3,658 m (12,000 ft), there is less oxygen, and they need to carry their own. High-altitude balloonists travel in pressurized cabins. At 19.31 km (12 miles) above sea level, atmospheric pressure is so low that body fluids vapourize and force their way through membranes, such as eyes and mouths.

Earth's highest mountain, Everest, is 8,848 m (29,029 ft) above sea level

Space nations

PEOPLE FROM AROUND THE WORLD are involved in space exploration. The vast majority will never go anywhere near space, but it is a major part of their lives. Only a handful of the world's countries regularly launch vehicles into space, but many more countries are involved in the preparation and manufacture of spacecraft and technology. Others are involved in monitoring space activities, or in simply reaping the benefits of space exploration; from the knowledge they gain of the Universe, to the cheap and instant telephone calls they make via satellites. Some nations work alone, others pool financial resources, knowledge, and expertise. Sending an astronaut, a space probe, or a satellite into space is a billion-dollar venture, which is achieved by thousands of people, and which benefits hundreds of thousands more.

MISSION BADGE
Each flight carrying astronauts, or launching space probes, has a cloth badge 10 cm (3.94 in) across. It features a selection of pictures and words representing the mission. France was the first nation to have astronauts fly aboard Soviet and American spacecraft. Jean-Loup Chretien's stay aboard Salyut 7 in 1982 was marked by this badge.

Engine nozzle

Thruster rockets for fine control

UNITED STATES

APOLLO 18
America's Apollo 18 completed the first international space rendezvous when it manoeuvred toward the Soviet Soyuz 19 in 1975. It carried the docking adaptor to join the two craft.

КОСМОС ДЛЯ МИРА
COSMOS FOR PEACE

SOUNDS OF SPACE
Space exploration has inspired people around the world to paint, write, and compose. This two-record set was released in 1975 at the time of the Apollo-Soyuz docking as a celebration of Soviet space achievement. One record includes space-to-ground transmission. The second plays patriotic songs. One song is sung by Yuri Gagarin, who was the first man ever to go into space.

GETTING THERE
Metals and parts used in spacecraft are produced by many manufacturers, and brought together for assembly and testing. The completed craft is then transported to the launch site. A large piece of space equipment, such as this major part of the Ariane 5 rocket, is transported by water. Here, it is being pulled through a harbour on route to its launch site at Kourou in French Guiana, South America.

MISSION CONTROL, CHINA
China sent its first satellite Mao 1 into space in 1970. From 1986, it has been a commercial launcher for satellites of other nations. This picture shows mission control staff at the Xichang site practising launch procedure.

Giant dish provides telephone and television links

THE EARS OF THE WORLD
Ground stations around the world are listening into space. Giant dishes collect data transmitted by distant planetary probes, satellite observatories looking into space and monitoring Earth, and communication satellites providing telephone links and television pictures. This 12 m (39 ft 4 in) dish at Lhasa in Tibet is used for telecommunications.

INDIA IN SPACE
India launched its first satellite in 1980, becoming the seventh nation to launch a space rocket. This badge marks the flight of Indian astronaut Rakesh Sharma to the Salyut 7 space station in April 1984.

HEADLINE NEWS
Sending astronauts into space has become such a regular event that it is reported on the inside pages of a newspaper, if at all. But when a country's first astronaut is launched, it makes headline news. The flight of the first astronaut from Poland, Miroslaw Hermaszewski, in 1978, and of the first Cuban, Arnaldo Tamayo Mendez, in 1980, were celebrated in their national press.

Docking adaptor

SOYUZ 19
Soyuz 19 was launched first, from the Soviet Union, a few hours before Apollo 18 left America. During docking, Soyuz kept pointing at Apollo and rolled to match its movement.

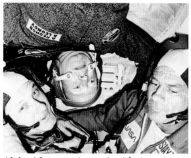

INTERNATIONAL RENDEZVOUS
In 1975, Americans and Soviets linked up for the first time in space. Three American astronauts aboard Apollo 18, and two Soviets on Soyuz 19, flew in tandem as they orbited the world. Once docked on 17 July, they stayed together for two days. Since the 1990s, the Americans and Russians have worked together regularly in space, first on Mir, and later on the International Space Station (ISS).

Aleksei Leonov (centre) with Americans Thomas Stafford and Donald Slayton

WELCOME GIFT
International space crews exchange gifts. Russians sometimes give sweets like these. Space crew aboard Mir greeted visiting astronauts with a traditional Russian gift of bread and salt as the visitors entered the space station. On Earth, the white floury bread is broken and eaten after dipping it in roughly-cut salt. The food had been adapted into prepackaged bread and salt wafers for space travel.

Prunariu's mission badge, showing flag of Romania

Gurragcha's mission badge, showing flag of Mongolia

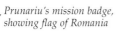

ROMANIA IN SPACE
Dumitru Prunariu was the first Romanian to enter space when he flew on Soyuz 40 to the Salyut 6 space station in May 1981. Along with astronaut Soviet Leonid Popov, Prunariu underwent psychological and medical tests. The custom of photographing the visiting astronaut's country was carried out as the station passed over Romania in daylight.

SEARCHING MONGOLIA
The eighth international crew on board a Soviet space station included Mongolian astronaut Jugderdemidiyn Gurragcha, who was on board Salyut 6 for eight days in March 1981. He carried out a number of experiments. Using mapping and other cameras, he searched for possible ore and petroleum deposits in Mongolia.

Rocket science

A ROCKET IS NEEDED to launch anything and anyone into space. It provides the power to lift itself and its cargo off the ground and, in a short space of time, the power to attain the speed which will carry it away from gravity's pull and into space. The burning rocket fuels produce hot gases that are expelled through an exhaust nozzle at the bottom of the rocket. This provides the force that lifts the vehicle off the ground. The space rocket was developed in the first half of the 20th century. Typically two rockets a week are launched into space from somewhere in the world.

EARLY ROCKETS
The earliest rockets were used by the Chinese about a thousand years ago. They were powered with gunpowder. Once ignited, an explosive burst propelled the rocket forward. They resembled firework rockets but were used as weapons. This 17th-century man shot rocket arrows from a basket.

ROCKET PIONEER
Konstantin Tsiolkovsky, a Soviet, started working on the theory of rocket space flight in the 1880s. He worked out how fast a rocket needed to go and how much fuel it would require. He proposed using liquid fuel, and using fuel in several stages.

ROCKET ENGINE
This is just one of four Viking engines that powered the Ariane 1 rocket – seen from below as it stands on the launch pad. In under two and a half minutes, and 50 km (31 miles) above the launch pad, its job was over.

Giant Viking rocket engine

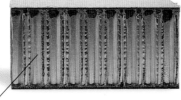

Honeycomb material is light and strong

Honeycomb structure is visible from the top

MADE TO MEASURE
The materials used in rockets and their cargoes need to be light. This is because a lighter rocket needs less fuel to launch it, and so it is less costly. The materials also need to be strong and able to withstand the thrust at launch. Some widely available materials such as steel are used. Others, like this honeycomb material, are specially developed and manufactured by rocket scientists and space engineers.

Nozzle where gases produced by burning fuel in booster rocket are expelled

Pipe delivers oxygen to hydrogen for combustion

Flags of nations involved in Ariane 5 project

25 tonnes of liquid hydrogen stored in tank placed here

Solid rocket boosters supply 90 per cent of thrust at liftoff

130 tonnes of liquid oxygen are stored in separate tank

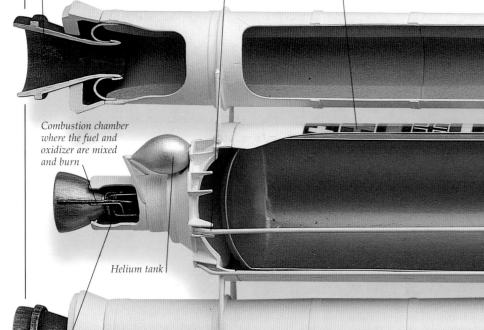

Combustion chamber where the fuel and oxidizer are mixed and burn

Helium tank

Liftoff procedure starts with the ignition of this Vulcain engine

French Space Agency emblem

Two boosters are ignited before the main rocket to supply initial thrust

European Space Agency (ESA) emblem

French rocket-manufacturing company (Arianespace) emblem

LIQUID-FUEL ROCKET
American Robert Goddard was fascinated by the idea of space travel. He experimented with rockets and different fuels. He launched the first ever liquid-fuel rocket in 1926. The flight lasted two and a half seconds and the rocket reached an altitude of 12.5 m (41 ft).

ROCKET POST
Enterprising ways of using rocket power were developed in the 1930s. These cards were sent across Germany by rocket post in 1931. They were specially produced cards, using special rocket post stamps. Ventures such as this one were short-lived.

ROCKET CAR
Fuel for use in rockets was tested in cars, rail vehicles, air gliders, and ice sledges in the 1920s. The cars resembled a rocket in shape and in the noise they made as they used the fuel. They either used liquid fuel or powdered solid fuel. The men who built and drove the cars were members of the newly formed German Society for Space Travel.

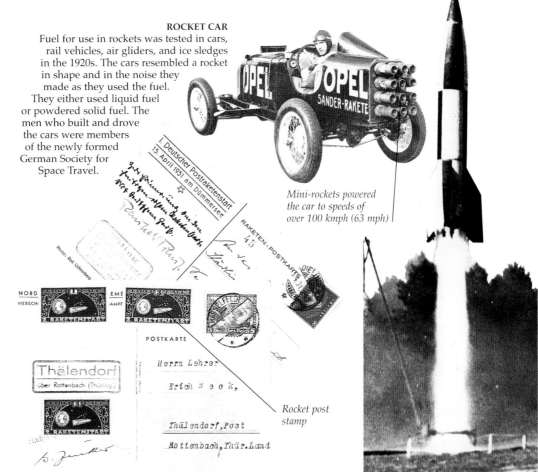

Mini-rockets powered the car to speeds of over 100 kmph (63 mph)

Rocket post stamp

ISLAND TO SPACE
Japan's Tanegashima space centre is one of over 20 launch sites around the world where rockets start their space journeys. From this island site, the Japanese space agency assembles, tests, launches, and keeps track of satellites. Japan became the fourth nation into space when it launched their first satellite in 1970. Launch sites are built close to Earth's equator to benefit from an extra push from the Earth's spin at launch.

FIRST TO SPACE
The V2 rocket was developed in Germany in the 1930s. Its first successful launch was in 1942, and it became the first mass-produced long-range rocket. It was first used as a weapon. Over 4,000 were fired in the last year of World War II against Britain. After the war, the V2 and subsequent rockets for space travel were developed by an American team headed by Wernher von Braun.

Parachute in nose cone for slow descent

Engine and fuel to move the pair of satellites into the correct orbit

Up to four satellites, like this one, can be carried into space

ARIANE 5
The Ariane rocket is the launch vehicle of the European Space Agency (ESA). The agency is made up of 15 European countries that fund and develop satellites and experiments for space. Over 140 satellites have been launched by the Ariane rocket from the ESA launch site at Kourou in French Guiana. The latest of the Ariane series, Ariane 5, is the most powerful. It is therefore able to launch heavy single satellites, or a few smaller ones. It has also been designed to allow astronauts to be transported in a specially modified upper stage.

Reusable rocket

When the first space shuttle was launched in 1981, it marked a turning point in space travel. Conventional one-use rockets had until then been the only way of sending astronauts or cargoes to space. If space travel was to become a regular event, a reusable system was needed. The United States came up with the answer in the form of the Space Transportation System (STS), or shuttle, for short. It is launched like a conventional rocket but returns to Earth like a plane. This means that two of its three main parts are used over and over again. Shuttles transport crew and equipment to the International Space Station (ISS), launch, retrieve, and repair satellites, launch space probes, and are used as space laboratories.

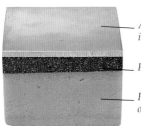

PIGGY BACK
When a shuttle orbiter (space plane) needs to be moved to a launch site, it is transported piggy-back style on top of a specially adapted Boeing 747 aircraft. The orbiter's rocket motors are protected by an aerodynamic tail-cover. The shuttle is then prepared for launch and is fitted with boosters and fuel tank for take off.

BLASTOFF
Within two minutes of the shuttle lifting off from the launch pad, the booster rockets are discarded, as is the fuel tank six minutes later. From liftoff to space takes less than ten minutes. Since the first launch in 1981, there have been over 100 successful flights. Atlantis' launch, shown here, in October 1985 was the 21st shuttle mission.

Aluminium inner structure

Foam coating

Protective outer layer

SAFE INSIDE
The shuttle's aluminium fuel tank is higher than a 15-storey building. It has been specially designed to carry and protect its cargo. Inside its outer layer, shown here, are two pressurized tanks that contain liquid hydrogen and liquid oxygen. During launch, the fuel is fed to the orbiter's three main engines.

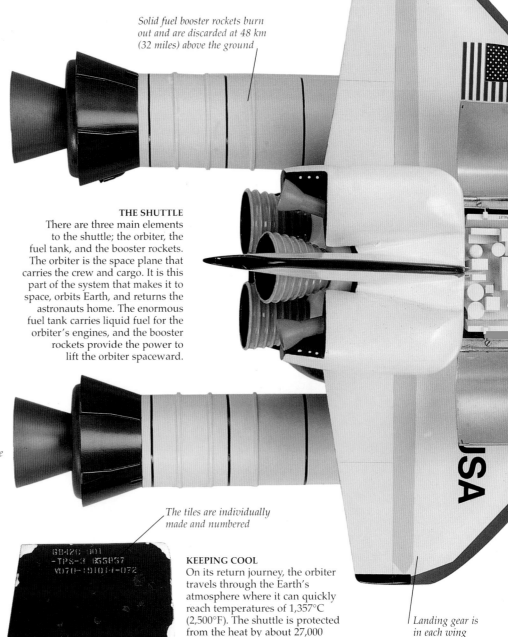

Solid fuel booster rockets burn out and are discarded at 48 km (32 miles) above the ground

THE SHUTTLE
There are three main elements to the shuttle; the orbiter, the fuel tank, and the booster rockets. The orbiter is the space plane that carries the crew and cargo. It is this part of the system that makes it to space, orbits Earth, and returns the astronauts home. The enormous fuel tank carries liquid fuel for the orbiter's engines, and the booster rockets provide the power to lift the orbiter spaceward.

The tiles are individually made and numbered

KEEPING COOL
On its return journey, the orbiter travels through the Earth's atmosphere where it can quickly reach temperatures of 1,357°C (2,500°F). The shuttle is protected from the heat by about 27,000 heat absorbent tiles fitted to the outside and a reinforced carbon compound on the nose and wings.

Landing gear is in each wing and under the orbiter's nose

HYPERSONIC AIRCRAFT

During the 1960s, the X-15 rocket-powered aircraft was used to investigate flight at hypersonic speeds. It was released at high altitude where the rocket motors were ignited. The pilot controlled the X-15 at about 6,500 kmph (4,062 mph). Experience gained with this craft was used in the design of the shuttle.

On board is Sally Ride, the first American female astronaut

ORBITER IN FLIGHT

There are currently four orbiters in the United States' shuttle fleet – Columbia, Discovery, Atlantis, and Endeavour. The orbiter Challenger is shown here on its second flight in June 1983. Challenger flew nine times before exploding just after liftoff in 1986.

SHUTTLE ASTRONAUTS

Each shuttle has a commander responsible for the whole flight, a pilot to help fly the orbiter, and a number of astronaut specialists. Mission specialists are in charge of the orbiter's systems and perform spacewalks. Payload specialists, who are not necessarily regular astronauts, work with particular equipment or experiments on board.

Commander John Young (left) and pilot Robert Crippen in training for the first ever shuttle flight

Payload bay doors open in flight

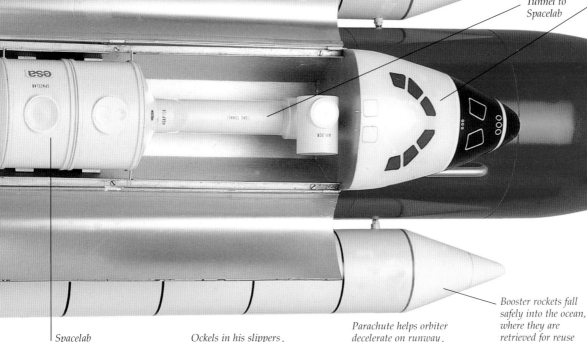

Tunnel to Spacelab

Flight deck and crew quarters for up to eight astronauts

External fuel tank is emptied in the first eight and a half minutes of flight. It is discarded and breaks up in the atmosphere

Spacelab

Ockels in his slippers

Parachute helps orbiter decelerate on runway

Booster rockets fall safely into the ocean, where they are retrieved for reuse

INSIDE SPACELAB

Wubbo Ockels, Dutch astronaut, was a payload specialist on Challenger's third mission in 1985. He worked inside Spacelab during the seven-day flight. There were 75 experiments on board, several of which were designed to give scientists data on how space travel affects the human body (pp. 28–29).

SHUTTLE LANDING

An orbiter's on-board motors are used to manoeuvre in space and to place it ready to come out of orbit and decelerate. The orbiter enters the atmosphere at 24,000 kmph (15,000 mph), slowing all the time. A loss of communications then follows for 12–16 minutes. Then the orbiter touches down on the runway at 344 kmph (215 mph), coming to rest after 2.4 km (1.5 miles).

The race for space

TWO NATIONS DOMINATED one of the most intense and successful periods of space exploration. For around 15 years, centred on the 1960s, America and the Soviet Union raced against each other to achieve success in space. Each wanted to make notable firsts: to be the first to put a satellite, and then a man, into space; to have the first astronaut in orbit and the first woman space traveller; to make the first spacewalk outside a craft; and to be the first to step on the Moon. The race got under way when the Soviets launched Sputnik 1, proving their space capability to the surprised Americans. From then on, each leapt forward in turn as new space achievements were made one after another.

UNITED CIGARETTES
These cigarettes celebrate the docking of the American Apollo 18 and Soviet Soyuz 19 in space in July 1975.

Apollo–Soyuz union cigarettes were printed in American on one side and Russian on the other

Aluminium sphere 58 cm (1 ft 11 in) across with four antennae

SPUTNIK 1
The space age started on 4 October 1957 when the first artificial satellite was launched by the Soviets. The satellite helped scientists learn more about the nature of Earth's uppermost atmosphere. As it orbited Earth every 96 minutes, its two radio transmitters signalled "bleep bleep".

EXPLORER 1
The rocket that was to carry the first American satellite into space, Vanguard, exploded on the launch pad. However, the satellite, Explorer 1, was already being constructed and, on 31 January 1958, it became the first American satellite in space. The Van Allen radiation belts surrounding Earth were discovered using scientific equipment on board.

Explorer 1 orbited Earth for 12 years

Service module was jettisoned before re-entry into Earth's atmosphere

Electrodes were attached to Laika to monitor her heart and breathing

Luna 3 transmitted the first views of the far side of the Moon

LUNA 3
In 1959, the first of the Luna series of craft was launched by the Soviets. Luna 1 was the first spacecraft to leave Earth's gravity. Luna 9 was the first craft to make a successful landing on the Moon. The Soviets also sent the first of their Venera series to Venus in 1961.

LAIKA, THE FIRST CREATURE IN SPACE
Only one month after the launch of Sputnik 1, the Soviets launched the first living creature into space aboard Sputnik 2. A dog called Laika travelled in a padded pressurized compartment and survived for a few days. The satellite was much heavier than anything the Americans were planning and suggested the Soviets were considering putting humans in orbit. American pride was injured and space became a political issue. The Americans resolved to enter and win the race.

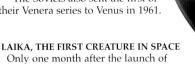

APOLLO 11
In the early 1960s, 377,000 Americans worked to get a man on the Moon. Ten Gemini two-manned missions successfully showed that the Americans could spacewalk, spend time in space, and dock craft. These were all necessary for the next three-manned Apollo programme, the one that would take men to the Moon (pp. 22–23).

FIRST AMONG EQUALS
Yuri Gagarin became the first human in space on 12 April 1961. Strapped in his Vostok 1 capsule, he orbited Earth once before re-entering Earth's atmosphere. After 108 minutes in space, he ejected himself from the capsule and parachuted to Earth. With him here is Valentina Tereshkova, the first woman in space.

HERO'S WELCOME
Gagarin's countrymen turned out in force to welcome him home from space. They filled the enormous Red Square in the heart of Moscow. But Gagarin was not only a hero in the Soviet Union. In the months ahead, crowds turned out to greet him wherever he toured.

Three-manned crew worked and slept in the command module, the only part of the mission to return to Earth

A PRESIDENT'S PROMISE
In the late 1950s, America increased space research funding and formed a space agency, NASA (National Aeronautics and Space Administration). Their first goal was to place a man in space. The Soviets beat them to it by one month. But in May 1961, America's new president, John F Kennedy, set a new goal of "landing a man on the Moon and returning him safely to the Earth" before the decade was out.

FIRST SPACEWALK
Once humans had successfully flown into space, both the Soviets and the Americans prepared to let them move outside their craft in space. The first EVA (extra vehicular activity), or spacewalk, was made by Soviet Aleksei Leonov in March 1965. He spent 24 minutes in space outside his Voskhod 2 spacecraft.

Command and service modules where crew is located

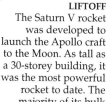

LIFTOFF
The Saturn V rocket was developed to launch the Apollo craft to the Moon. As tall as a 30-storey building, it was the most powerful rocket to date. The majority of its bulk was fuel. The top third of the rocket consisted of the lunar module for landing on the Moon; the service module providing the oxygen, water, and power for the crew; and, right on top, the command module.

THE MOON TO MEXICO
Michael Collins (left), Buzz Aldrin (rear), and Neil Armstrong of Apollo 11, the first mission to land a man on the Moon, are greeted in Mexico City. The three visited 24 countries in 45 days as part of a goodwill tour after their safe return from the Moon. One million people had turned up in Florida, USA, to see the start of their journey, but many more welcomed them home. Collins orbited the Moon in the command module while the others explored the lunar surface.

Space travellers

Around 400 people and countless other living creatures have travelled from Earth into space. All but 26 of them, men who went to the Moon, have spent their time in space in a craft orbiting Earth. Competition to travel into space is keen. When a call for potential European astronauts was made in the early 1990s, 20,000 people applied, six of whom were chosen for training. Astronauts are men and women with an outstanding ability in a scientific discipline, who are both mentally and physically fit. Originally, animals went into space to test the conditions prior to the first human flight. Now, along with insects and birds, they accompany astronauts, and are used for scientific research.

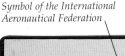

Symbol of the International Aeronautical Federation

Passport requests, in five languages, that any necessary help be given to the holder

Photograph of Helen Sharman, British astronaut and owner of this passport

№ 087

PASSPORT TO SPACE
A passport is carried for space travel in case it is needed when the astronaut returns to Earth. An unscheduled landing may be made in a country other than that of the launch. The type shown here is carried by astronauts on Russian craft. The term astronaut describes space travellers from all countries. But those on board Russian craft are also called cosmonauts.

Belka

UNTETHERED FLIGHT
Astronauts venturing outside their spacecraft need to be tethered to the craft, or to wear an MMU, manned manoeuvring unit. It is a powered backpack for travelling free in space. Without it, the astronaut would be "lost" in his own orbit around Earth.

American Bruce McCandless makes first spacewalk using a hand-controlled MMU, in 1984

Ham, the first chimpanzee astronaut, or "chimpnaut"

Strelka

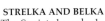

HAM
Chimpanzees were chosen for space travel because of their similar genetic make up to humans, and because they could be trained to perform tasks. Ham was the first to travel in January 1961. On his return, he was examined and found to be in excellent condition.

STRELKA AND BELKA
The Soviets launched a number of four-legged astronauts into space. The first living thing to travel from Earth was the dog, Laika, in 1957 (pp. 18–19). She perished in flight, but two other dogs, Strelka and Belka, returned safely to Earth by parachute in August 1960.

HONEYBEES
In April, 1984, a comb of honeybees travelled aboard the space shuttle Challenger. Like most travellers into space, the bees found weightlessness confusing to start with. But, once they had found their "space wings", they built their hive as successfully as they do on Earth.

Frog is placed in capsule for flight

SPINNING FROGS
Over 25 years ago, two bullfrogs orbited Earth to help medical research into the workings of the human inner ear. The frogs were monitored over a five-day period in both weightless and partial-gravity conditions. The frogs were spun in their capsule to create the partial gravity.

SQUIRREL MONKEY
The first monkey into space was a squirrel monkey, Gordo, in December 1958. Since then dogs, monkeys, flies, fish, ants, frogs, sea urchins, and over 2,000 jellyfish have been some of the creatures to travel to space. They have been used for research into various subjects, including the effects of weightlessness, fertility, and reproduction.

Animal and human crews have backups, reserves in case one of the original crew falls sick. This monkey backup is drinking some juice

A mask provides oxygen for breathing

Hector, a white rat, was launched from France

READY FOR SPACE
Early animal travellers wore their own spacesuits. Several suits were tested by the Soviets to see which would give their astronaut dogs the most protection. The dogs were chosen because their blood circulation and respiration are close to our own, and they were patient creatures.

WHITE RAT
Mice and rats have travelled into space for over 40 years. One of the first, Hector, a white rat, soared 161 km (100 miles) into space in 1961, and landed safely back on Earth three minutes later, alive and well.

SPACE ZOO
Two monkeys, snails, beetles, and fruit midges travelled together in December 1996. After a two-week trip to space, they were tested for effects of weightlessness before returning to their Earth zoo. They were loaded on board the Vostok rocket in their own capsule. Bone tissue from the monkeys' hip bones, taken before and after the flight, was used for medical research. Monkeys going into space are named in Russian alphabetical order. The winners of a school competition named these two Lapik and Multik.

Man on the Moon

THE MOON IS THE ONLY WORLD that humans have landed on outside their own. For centuries, Earth's companion in space has aroused our interest and, as Earth's nearest neighbour, it was the most likely target for manned space travel. Between 1969 and 1972, twelve American astronauts touched down on the Moon. They travelled there in six separate Apollo missions and spent just over 300 hours on the Moon's surface – 80 hours of that outside the landing craft. They collected rock samples, took photographs, and set up experiments to monitor the Moon's activity and environment. The Apollo missions were followed worldwide.

Apollo 16 lunar module, code named Orion

Upper part of Orion, which is where astronauts lived while on Moon, rejoined command module for return journey

Landing legs remained behind when Orion blasted off the Moon and docked with the command module for the return journey

Lunar module is photographed from behind – entrance is on other side

American flag needed small telescopic arm to keep it extended on the airless Moon

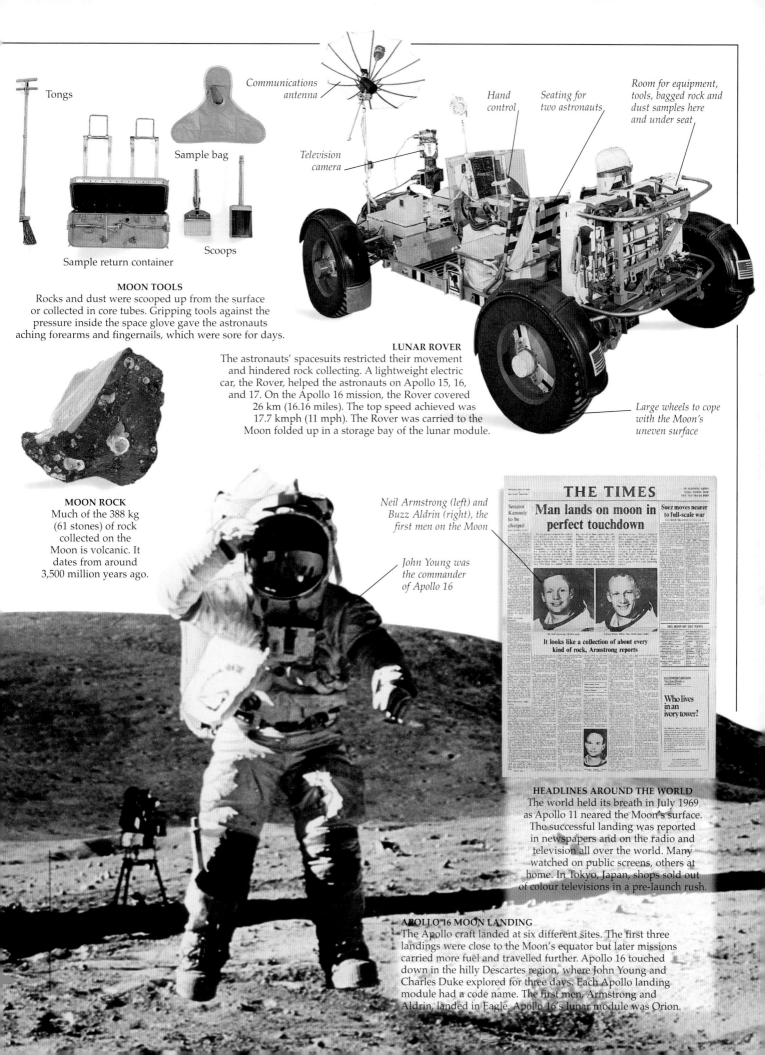

Tongs

Sample bag

Sample return container

Scoops

Communications antenna

Television camera

Hand control

Seating for two astronauts

Room for equipment, tools, bagged rock and dust samples here and under seat

MOON TOOLS

Rocks and dust were scooped up from the surface or collected in core tubes. Gripping tools against the pressure inside the space glove gave the astronauts aching forearms and fingernails, which were sore for days.

LUNAR ROVER

The astronauts' spacesuits restricted their movement and hindered rock collecting. A lightweight electric car, the Rover, helped the astronauts on Apollo 15, 16, and 17. On the Apollo 16 mission, the Rover covered 26 km (16.16 miles). The top speed achieved was 17.7 kmph (11 mph). The Rover was carried to the Moon folded up in a storage bay of the lunar module.

Large wheels to cope with the Moon's uneven surface

MOON ROCK

Much of the 388 kg (61 stones) of rock collected on the Moon is volcanic. It dates from around 3,500 million years ago.

Neil Armstrong (left) and Buzz Aldrin (right), the first men on the Moon

John Young was the commander of Apollo 16

THE TIMES

Senator Kennedy to be charged

Man lands on moon in perfect touchdown

Suez moves nearer to full-scale war

It looks like a collection of about every kind of rock, Armstrong reports

Who lives in an ivory tower?

HEADLINES AROUND THE WORLD

The world held its breath in July 1969 as Apollo 11 neared the Moon's surface. The successful landing was reported in newspapers and on the radio and television all over the world. Many watched on public screens, others at home. In Tokyo, Japan, shops sold out of colour televisions in a pre-launch rush.

APOLLO 16 MOON LANDING

The Apollo craft landed at six different sites. The first three landings were close to the Moon's equator but later missions carried more fuel and travelled further. Apollo 16 touched down in the hilly Descartes region, where John Young and Charles Duke explored for three days. Each Apollo landing module had a code name. The first men, Armstrong and Aldrin, landed in Eagle. Apollo 16's lunar module was Orion.

How to be an astronaut

SUSPENDED
As well as learning about spacecraft systems and the theory of working in space, astronauts must practise tasks in space conditions. They can learn what it is like to be in weightless conditions by scuba training or by using equipment like this harness which helps an astronaut get used to floating free.

MEN AND WOMEN ARE CHOSEN from around the world to train for travelling in space. They are launched aboard either the American shuttle, where English is the main language, or the Russian Soyuz rocket, where Russian is spoken. The preparations of the two space crews are similar and involve classroom and practical training, including work in mock-ups of the orbiter and parts of the International Space Station (ISS) and in simulators such as the harness, the "5DF" machine, the moon-walker, and the multi-axis wheel, examples of which are found at the Euro Space Center, Transinne, Belgium, and are shown on these two pages. Astronauts can be selected for training every two years. They have a year's basic training, followed by training related to an astronaut's role in space, such as a pilot or mission specialist, who performs extra vehicular activity (EVA). Only then do the successful astronauts get assigned to a flight.

Harness helps astronaut get used to floating free

Three Apollo astronauts in training before their flights to the Moon

JUNGLE EMERGENCY
Astronauts are trained for any kind of situation or emergency. These astronauts are gathering leaves and branches to make a shelter after a pretend emergency landing in the middle of the Panama jungle. Even after landing on Earth, an astronaut's journey may not be over.

LIFE RAFT
Astronaut candidates receive training in parachute jumping and land and sea survival. American astronaut Leroy Chiao floats in his life raft in training for an emergency departure from the space shuttle.

MOON-WALKER
Walking in a bulky spacesuit is difficult, particularly on the Moon where gravity is one-sixth of Earth's. The Apollo astronauts found bunny hops the best way to get around the lunar surface. Future trips to the Moon or to Mars can be prepared for by walking in a moon-walker, a suspended chair.

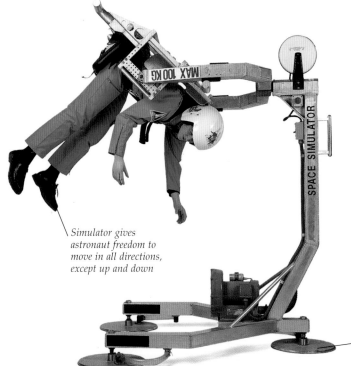

Simulator gives astronaut freedom to move in all directions, except up and down

Three "feet" float over the floor simulating movement achieved in frictionless space

FIVE DEGREES OF FREEDOM
Preparing for the weightlessness of space is not easy. The feeling can be simulated in a chair called the Five Degrees of Freedom (5DF) machine, which allows the astronaut to move in all directions, other than up and down, without restraint. Alternatively, astronauts can get a 20- to 30-second taste of weightlessness aboard a modified KC-135 jet aircraft as it dives from 10,668 m (35,000 ft) to 7,315 m (24,000 ft). But the experience is brief, even though it can be repeated up to 40 times a day.

UNDERWATER WEIGHTLESSNESS
Spacesuited astronauts can train for EVA in large water tanks, where the sensation of gravity is reduced. Space shuttle astronauts train with full-scale models of the orbiter payload bay and various payloads. Here some engineers work on a space station mock-up in preparation for future missions.

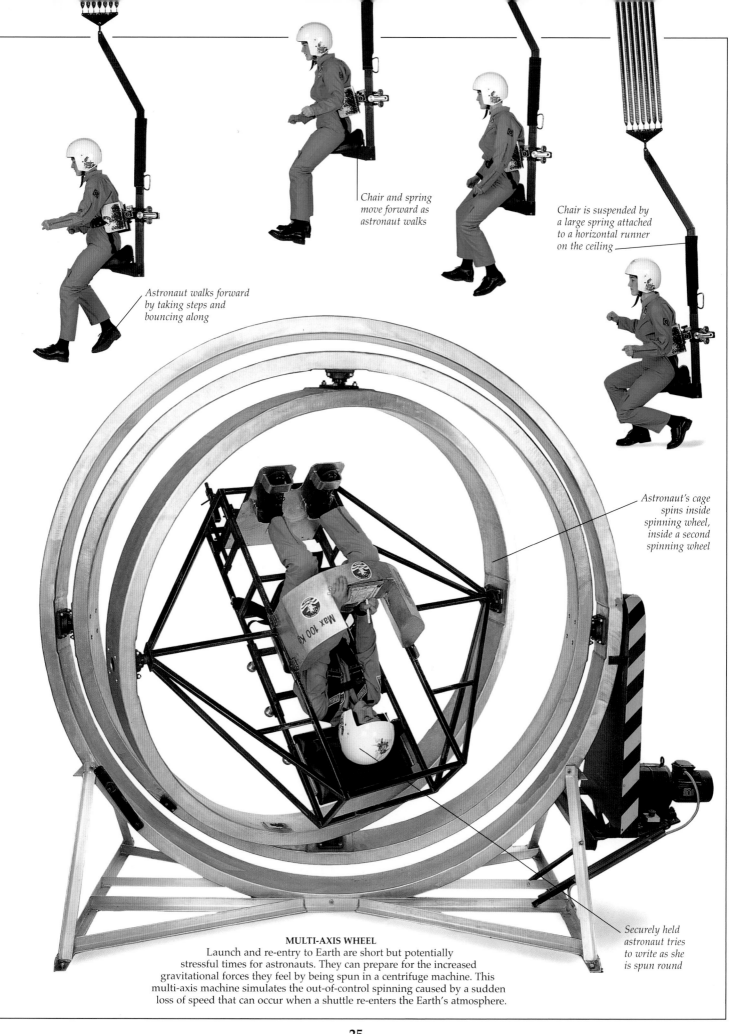

Chair and spring move forward as astronaut walks

Astronaut walks forward by taking steps and bouncing along

Chair is suspended by a large spring attached to a horizontal runner on the ceiling

Astronaut's cage spins inside spinning wheel, inside a second spinning wheel

Securely held astronaut tries to write as she is spun round

Max 100 kg

MULTI-AXIS WHEEL
Launch and re-entry to Earth are short but potentially stressful times for astronauts. They can prepare for the increased gravitational forces they feel by being spun in a centrifuge machine. This multi-axis machine simulates the out-of-control spinning caused by a sudden loss of speed that can occur when a shuttle re-enters the Earth's atmosphere.

Astronaut fashion

A SPACESUIT IS LIKE a protective, portable tent that an astronaut wears to shield him in space. The first suits were designed for astronauts who were simply flying through space without leaving their craft. The suit they were launched in stayed on during eating, sleeping, going to the toilet, and the return journey. Next came the suit for space itself. This provided the astronaut with a life support system and protection against temperature extremes and space dust. Before going outside, the suit is pressurized to guard against the near vacuum of space. Today's astronauts wear suits for launch, work outside, and return. Inside, they wear casual, Earthly clothes.

Urine transferred from here

MOBILE MAN
The first spacesuits were based on high altitude jet aircraft pressure suits. Astronauts wearing them had to be able to bend their arms and legs. The Apollo suits for the Moon had bellow-like moulded rubber joints. The design has been simplified in this toy from 1966.

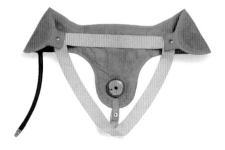

Male underpants, designed for thermal control, 1960s

Device for collecting urine for male astronauts, early 1960s

SPACE UNDERWEAR
Coping with human waste presents a tricky design problem. Any collecting device needs to keep the astronaut comfortable but dry at the same time. Collecting devices were essential for astronauts on early craft without toilets and, today, for long periods spent outside the craft.

Portable life support system

Suit of Yuri Gagarin, first man in space, in 1961

Aleksei Leonov's suit, the first to be used outside spacecraft, in 1965

Oleg Makarov's suit used between 1973 and 1980

Mir space station suit used in the late 1980s

All-in-one overshoe with sole and heel

CHANGING FASHION
A spacesuit's main job is to protect an astronaut. But it must also allow him to move about easily. These two basic requirements have not changed since the first astronaut flew. Yet, as the suits here show, spacesuit design has changed. New materials and techniques and practical experience combine to produce a comfortable and efficient suit for today's working astronaut. A suit is no longer tailor-made for one person but off-the-peg, and can be reused by another astronaut.

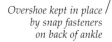

Overshoe kept in place by snap fasteners on back of ankle

Oxygen passed to helmet through channels in internal surface

Visor's gold coating reflected heat and light

Outer helmet

Pressure helmet

Communications cap

Pen-light pocket

DESIGNED FOR THE MOON
The Apollo suits were designed for use on the Moon. Closest to the skin, the astronaut wore a one-piece lightweight garment with sensors for monitoring changes in his body. Next was a garment with a network of 91.44 m (300 ft) of tubing with constantly circulating cool water to maintain the astronaut's correct body heat. On top came the suit made of high-strength synthetic fibres, metals, and plastics. A portable life support system was added on the back and controlled from the chest of the suit when the astronauts went outside their craft.

Two-piece underwear of long sleeved vest and full length pants

One-piece suit and underwear worn under spacesuit for launch and return home

Flag of Great Britain

Unisex one-piece has under-leg zip for quicker waste removal

Outer glove placed over an inner pressure glove

IN-FLIGHT SPACE CLOTHES
Astronauts now have a selection of clothes they can wear inside a spacecraft. In the warm, safe atmosphere of a shuttle orbiter or a space station, astronauts wear unisex t-shirts and shorts or jogging style trousers. Socks keep feet warm, but there is no need for shoes. Helen Sharman's in-flight clothes included this one-piece sleeveless suit and jacket. In fact it was far too warm on Mir to wear them together when she stayed on the station in 1991.

GEMINI SUIT
A member of the team who designed and made the suits for the American astronauts in the 1960s tests out a Gemini suit. It was worn by the first Americans to walk in space outside their craft.

Outer layers offer protection against temperature extremes and space dust

Foot straps hold trousers in place

Pocket contents secured by zip fastener

Living in space

ALL THE THINGS THAT WE DO on Earth to stay alive are also done by astronauts in space. Astronauts still need to eat, breathe, sleep, keep clean and healthy, and use the toilet. Everything needed for these activities is transported to, or made in, space. The main difference between life on Earth and in space is weightlessness. Seemingly simple, everyday tasks, such as breathing inside the craft, need to be carefully thought out. As the astronauts use up oxygen and breathe out carbon dioxide, they are in danger of suffocating. Fresh oxygen is circulated round the craft. Water vapour from the astronauts' breath is collected and recycled for use in experiments and for drinking. Air is used rather than water to suck, and not flush, body wastes away.

WITHOUT SETTLING
Anything not tied down in a spacecraft will move around with the slightest push. Dust does not settle and so must be vacuumed out of the air.

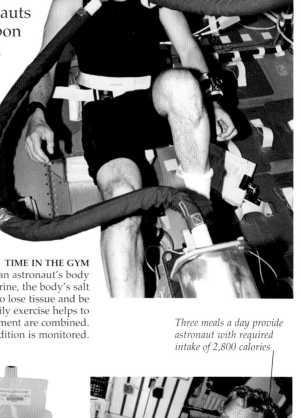

UNDER PRESSURE
Body fluids are no longer pulled down by gravity and move up towards an astronaut's head. For the first few days, his face looks fatter and his nasal passages are blocked. Belts worn at the top of each leg help control the flow until the body adjusts itself.

TIME IN THE GYM
The upward movement of fluids in an astronaut's body causes the kidneys to excrete more urine, the body's salt concentration to be upset, and muscles to lose tissue and be less able to work. About two hours of daily exercise helps to counteract this. Here exercise and experiment are combined. As Canadian Robert Thirsk pedals, his condition is monitored.

Three meals a day provide astronaut with required intake of 2,800 calories

Pineapple

Peach

Tea w/Lemon & Artificial Sweetener

Lemon-Lime Drink

Drinks

Sweet and sour beef

Pear

Rice

Fruit and nuts

Chicken

WHAT'S ON THE MENU?
Meals are prepared long before launch. Packaged foods are either ready to eat, need warming, or need water to be added. Many foods, such as cornflakes, meatballs, and lemon pudding, are similar to those on a supermarket shelf. Fresh foods are eaten at the start of a trip or when delivered by visiting astronauts.

Cereals

Food packages held on tray, which is strapped to astronaut's leg

Peas

Almonds

Holes in the cutlery handles mean they can be tied down

PERSONAL HYGIENE

Astronauts who flew to Mir were given a material pouch containing personal hygiene items. This one was issued to British astronaut Helen Sharman for her stay on board Mir in 1991. Individual pockets contain hair-, teeth-, and hand-care items. Teeth are cleaned with a brush and edible, non-frothy toothpaste, or with an impregnated finger wipe.

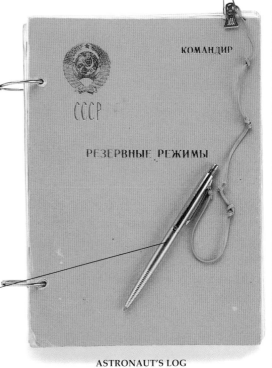

In pens designed for space, ink is pushed towards nib. On Earth gravity pulls ink down

ASTRONAUT'S LOG

An astronaut's log book contains details of flight procedures. Helen Sharman followed the launch, Mir-docking, and Earth-landing in hers. She flew to Mir on the Russian craft Soyuz TM-12. As part of her training, she had learnt to speak Russian.

HIGH-FLYING BUTTERFLY

Everything an astronaut might need in space is provided by the space agency he or she is flying with. But astronauts do have the chance of taking a personal item or two with them. These must be small and light. Helen Sharman carried this brooch given to her by her father.

Body-washing wipe

SPACE SHOWER

The first private toilet and shower were on the American space station Skylab, which was in space in 1973–4. The toilet was unreliable and disturbed other astronauts when in use. The shower proved leaky, and astronauts spent precious time cleaning up. The Americans decided to do without one in the shuttle system, and the one on Mir is rarely used.

KEEPING CLEAN

Wet wipes are used to clean astronauts' bodies and the inside of the spacecraft. Some, like these Russian ones, are specially made for use in space. Others are commercial baby wipes.

American astronaut Jack Lousma uses shower on Skylab

Inside sealed unit, water is air-blasted at astronaut and immediately sucked up

Handle for astronaut to hold himself down

WASTE MANAGEMENT

On entering the toilet, an astronaut puts on a rubber glove and chooses a funnel. Once this is fitted to the waste hose, he sits down and holds the funnel close to his body. The toilet fan is turned on and, as the astronaut urinates, the liquid is drawn through the hose by air. Before discarding solid waste, the toilet bowl is pressurized to produce a tight seal between the astronaut and the seat. Finally, the astronaut cleans himself, and the toilet, with wipes.

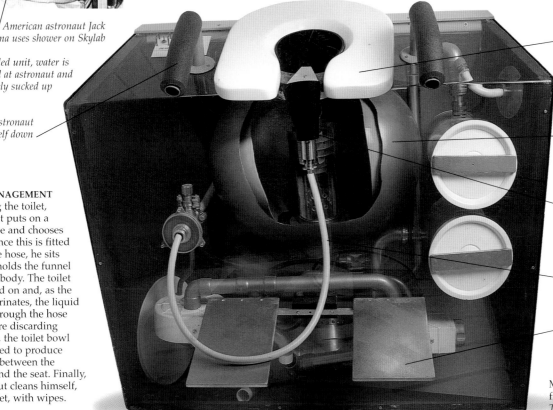

Astronaut sits here, toilet seat is lifted up for cleaning

Toilet is cut away to show how the solid waste is collected

Male or female funnel is held close to the astronaut to collect liquid waste

Hose takes away liquid waste

Feet are secured on the footrests

Model of space toilet from *Euro Space Center, Transinne, Belgium*

Astronauts at work

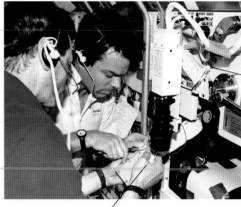

A WORKING DAY FOR AN ASTRONAUT could be spent inside or outside his craft. Inside, routine monitoring and maintenance on the craft is carried out alongside scientific testing and experimentation. This can include investigation of the effects of space travel on the human body, testing of new products in space, and research into food production, which will benefit future space generations. Commercial organizations send experiments into space to be performed in weightlessness. Work outside is called extra vehicular activity (EVA). An astronaut will either be tethered to his craft or wear a manned manoeuvring unit (MMU) – a powered backpack. He might deploy satellites, set up experiments, or help build the International Space Station (ISS).

Repair of the "Bubble Drop Particle Unit"

RUNNING REPAIRS
In-flight repairs had to be made to an experiment unit on board Columbia. Back on Earth, Spanish astronaut Pedro Duque carried out the very same repair procedure. His work was recorded, and the video pictures were transmitted to the in-flight crew, Frenchman Jean-Jacques Favier and American Kevin Kregel, who then carried out the real repair.

ORDERS FROM BELOW
Astronauts are assigned tasks on a mission long before they leave Earth. They work closely with the scientists and engineers who have designed and produced experiments in the months prior to launch. While the astronauts are in space, the scientists wait on Earth for the successful completion of the mission. Once they stayed in touch through the teleprinter, but laptops are more convenient today.

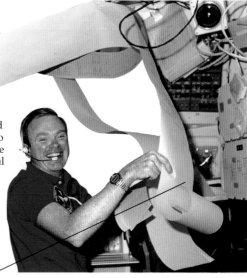

Goggles and headgear examine how astronaut orientates

American astronaut Richard Linnehan in Spacelab aboard Columbia

Challenger was filled with several football fields' length of paper in 1985

LOOK AFTER YOURSELF
For some work, the astronaut is both the scientist and the subject of his investigation. His job is to see how the human body – his own body – copes with the space environment. On Earth, gravity pulls things towards its surface and so provides a visual reference for up and down. In space, there is no up and down and this can be very disorientating.

Astronaut prepares samples in the glove box

WORKING IN A GLOVE BOX
Experiments from around the world have been carried out in Mir and in Spacelab (right), the European laboratory carried on the shuttle. Some only needed activating when in space, others needed more direct participation by an astronaut. American astronaut Leroy Chiao (top) places samples in one of the centrifuges on board. American Donald Thomas' hands are in the glove box, a sealed experiment unit.

Securing pins

Sheet cutters

Bolt tightener

Wire cutters

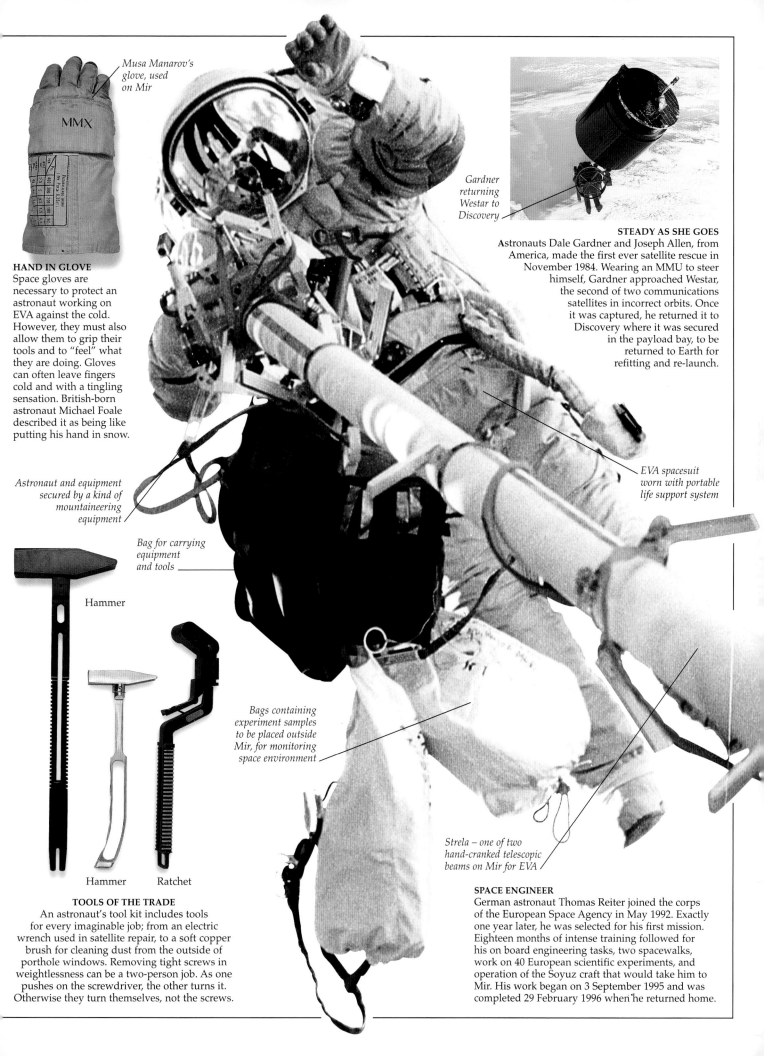

HAND IN GLOVE
Space gloves are necessary to protect an astronaut working on EVA against the cold. However, they must also allow them to grip their tools and to "feel" what they are doing. Gloves can often leave fingers cold and with a tingling sensation. British-born astronaut Michael Foale described it as being like putting his hand in snow.

Musa Manarov's glove, used on Mir

MMX

Astronaut and equipment secured by a kind of mountaineering equipment

Bag for carrying equipment and tools

Hammer

Hammer   Ratchet

TOOLS OF THE TRADE
An astronaut's tool kit includes tools for every imaginable job; from an electric wrench used in satellite repair, to a soft copper brush for cleaning dust from the outside of porthole windows. Removing tight screws in weightlessness can be a two-person job. As one pushes on the screwdriver, the other turns it. Otherwise they turn themselves, not the screws.

Bags containing experiment samples to be placed outside Mir, for monitoring space environment

Gardner returning Westar to Discovery

STEADY AS SHE GOES
Astronauts Dale Gardner and Joseph Allen, from America, made the first ever satellite rescue in November 1984. Wearing an MMU to steer himself, Gardner approached Westar, the second of two communications satellites in incorrect orbits. Once it was captured, he returned it to Discovery where it was secured in the payload bay, to be returned to Earth for refitting and re-launch.

EVA spacesuit worn with portable life support system

Strela – one of two hand-cranked telescopic beams on Mir for EVA

SPACE ENGINEER
German astronaut Thomas Reiter joined the corps of the European Space Agency in May 1992. Exactly one year later, he was selected for his first mission. Eighteen months of intense training followed for his on board engineering tasks, two spacewalks, work on 40 European scientific experiments, and operation of the Soyuz craft that would take him to Mir. His work began on 3 September 1995 and was completed 29 February 1996 when he returned home.

Rest and play

Yo-yo thrown out sideways comes back without gravity pulling it down

Astronauts have leisure time in space just as they would if they were down on Earth. When the day's work is finished, they might like to indulge in a favourite pastime of reading, photography, or music, or join together for a game of cards. Whatever their preference, they are bound to spend some time simply gazing out of the spacecraft window. Watching the world far below is a pastime no astronaut tires of. When the first astronauts went into space, they had every moment of their time accounted for and ground control was always listening in. Time to unwind and enjoy the experience and unique sensations space offers is now in every astronaut's timetable.

SEEING SHARKS
American astronaut Bill Lenoir watches his rubber shark.

REPUBLIQUE FRANCAISE
MEZIERES   POSTES 1988
LA COMMUNICATION   **2,20**

WRITING HOME
Lap top computers can help astronauts stay in touch with family and friends on a day-to-day basis. Others prefer to write letters home. Astronauts on Mir operated their own post office. Letters were stamped and dated when written and handed over when the astronaut got back to Earth. The French stamp for Earth-use celebrated communication.

Jacks float in midair as there is no gravity to keep them on a surface

A chain of seven magnetic marbles is achieved on Earth before gravity pulls them apart

In space, because the marbles are weightless, you can keep on adding to the chain

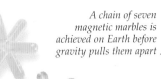

STAY STILL!
On Earth, jacks are picked up in increasing numbers from the floor as the ball is thrown up and caught. In space, the jacks are released in midair but always drift apart. The ball is thrown to a spacecraft wall and caught on its return journey.

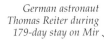

Drink flows out independently unless mouthpiece is sealed between sips

SNACKTIME
Hungry astronauts have a choice of food snacks and drink for in between meals. Dried fruit, nuts, crumb-free biscuit bars, and hot or cold drinks supplement their diet. Drinks are usually taken from sealed packs or tubes. Once this coke can is opened in space, the drink can flow out freely, so it needs a special mouthpiece.

Guitar collapses for easy storage

German astronaut Thomas Reiter during 179-day stay on Mir

COSMIC CHORDS
Music tapes are light and small, two important qualities for any non-essential item carried into space. Singing along can be fun, but as one astronaut relaxes, another is still working hard only feet away, so the volume cannot be too high. Sometimes a change of music is supplied by visiting astronauts. In November 1995, an Atlantis crew briefly docked with Mir, leaving behind a gift of a collapsible guitar.

SPACE TOYS

Ten familiar toys were packed aboard the space shuttle Discovery when it blasted into space in April 1985. These ten, plus one more the astronauts made in space, a paper aeroplane, became the stars of an educational video. The mid-deck became a classroom as the astronauts demonstrated the toys, including a yo-yo, jacks, and magnetic marbles.

Hair only moves upward if pushed

HAIR-RAISING

Washing clothes and hair are not top priorities in space. Clothes are bagged and brought home dirty. Hair washing can be avoided if the trip is short. If it needs to be washed, it cannot be done in the usual way with lots of water and shampoo. Dirt can be wiped away by a cloth impregnated with a shampoo-type substance.

American Susan Helms tests space shampoo

Inflatable ring provides support for the sleeping astronaut

Wubbo Ockels from the Netherlands on board space shuttle Challenger in 1985

SPACE PHOTOGRAPHER

Taking photographs in space is one way to keep a unique memory alive. Cameras for prints, slides, video, and movie film are on board the spacecraft. As well as making an official record of the trip, astronauts take fun shots. American Karl Henize photographs through the window of the Challenger shuttle orbiter to catch the scene in the payload bay outside.

Woolly slippers gave Ockels extra warmth and comfort

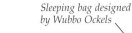

Sleeping bag designed by Wubbo Ockels

GOOD NIGHT, SLEEP TIGHT

Astronauts once slept in their seats or in temporarily hung hammocks. Today they have a more comfortable choice. Sleeping bags are attached to the sides of the spacecraft, or a sound suppression blanket and sheets with weightlessness restraints are used in a private bunk bed. This special sleeping bag was used in the 1980s aboard the space shuttle and Mir. Its inflatable ring simulates the pressure that the weight of bedclothes provides on Earth.

Danger and disaster

GREAT CARE IS TAKEN IN THE PLANNING and preparation of a space mission. Once a rocket and its cargo leaves the ground, there is little anyone can do if things go badly wrong. The smallest error can mean the end of a billion dollar project. Years of work and the hopes and expectations of hundreds of people can be lost in a second. Mistakes can happen and problems do arise. They range from an astronaut's cold that delayed a flight, through whole projects that failed, to the loss of life. But big disasters are rare and we are incredibly successful at sending craft and astronauts into space.

NEIGHBOURS
The American shuttle launch centre is in Florida, USA, next to a wildlife refuge. The osprey is one of over 300 species of birds in the area. Space technicians check regularly that the birds do not nest in the wrong place.

PARACHUTE PROBLEM
Vladimir Komarov was the first human to be killed in space flight. After a day in space, he descended to Earth on 24 April 1967. The lines of his Soyuz 1 parachute became tangled. The parachute deflated, the craft plunged to the ground and burst into flames.

The Apollo 13 crew are honoured. Their mission was regarded as a successful failure because of the rescue experience gained

President Nixon welcomes home the crew of Apollo 13

MISSION ABORT
On 13 April 1970, two days after launch, Apollo 13's journey to the Moon was interrupted when an oxygen tank ruptured and caused an explosion which damaged power and life support systems on board. The major incident was calmly reported to Earth with the words "Houston, we've had a problem here". The planned lunar landing was abandoned and every effort was channelled into getting the three-man crew home safely.

John Swigert   Fred Haise   James Lovell   Richard Nixon

HOME AT LAST
The explosion aboard Apollo 13 was in the service module and put its engine out of action. The astronauts used the engine of the lunar module, originally intended for manoeuvre on and off the Moon, to take them round the Moon and return them to Earth. Everyone was relieved as the astronauts were lifted aboard the recovery ship.

FLASH FIRE
Astronauts Virgil Grissom, Edward White, and Roger Chaffee perished in a fire in the command module of the American Apollo 1 on 27 January 1967. They were on the ground practising launch countdown. The astronauts could not open the module hatch to escape. Spacecraft were redesigned.

Effects of the intense heat can be seen on the outside of the command module

Urns holding the remains of the astronauts were placed in the Kremlin wall

RETURN FROM SPACE
After a 23-day stay aboard the Salyut 1 space station, Soviet astronauts Georgi Dobrovolsky, Vladislav Volkov, and Viktor Patsayev started their journey home. As they approached Earth on 30 June 1971, air escaped from their capsule. The three were not wearing spacesuits, suffocated, and were found dead when their capsule had landed.

Astronauts test launch pad emergency exit in a dress rehearsal for their launch

One of seven baskets. Each basket can hold three crew members and has its own wire system to carry them safely to the ground

Personalised badge was made to commemorate a teacher – rather than a regularly trained astronaut – going into space

Challenger, the space shuttle orbiter, first flew in 1983. This 1986 flight was its tenth mission into space

NASA stands for National Aeronautics and Space Administration, the American space agency. It flies the space shuttle

ESCAPE ROUTE

Emergency procedures have been developed to allow astronauts to get away from their craft quickly. For shuttle astronauts, the escape route before the final 30 seconds of countdown is via a steel-wire basket. It takes 35 seconds to slide to the ground, practised here. On arrival, the astronauts move to an emergency bunker until they get the all clear.

LOST IN SPACE

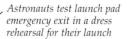

In February 1996, astronauts were putting a satellite into space when the 20.6 km (12.8 miles) tether that connected it to the space shuttle Columbia snapped. The US$ 442 million satellite had to be given up as lost. Astronauts had unsuccessfully tried to deploy the Italian satellite four years earlier. Once deployed, the satellite would have been swept through Earth's magnetic field to generate electricity.

CHALLENGER TRAGEDY

Seventy-three seconds after liftoff on 28 January 1986, the space shuttle Challenger exploded. All seven of the crew were killed, including teacher Sharon Christa McAuliffe. She had won a national contest in America to travel aboard the shuttle and was planning to take a class from space. Launch pad preparation and liftoff are among the most dangerous parts of a mission. This was the first flight to take off and not reach space.

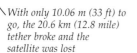

With only 10.06 m (33 ft) to go, the 20.6 km (12.8 mile) tether broke and the satellite was lost

Mars-96 was assembled at the Lavochkin Scientific-Industrial Association, Khimki, near Moscow

MARS-96

The Russian space probe Mars-96 was launched successfully from the Baikonur space centre on 16 November 1996, but, about half an hour after take off, contact with the probe was lost. The fourth set of boosters had failed to lift Mars-96 out of Earth orbit and onto its target, Mars.

PECKING PROBLEM

A yellow-shafted flicker woodpecker delayed the launch of the space shuttle in June 1995. Discovery was ready for liftoff on the launch pad but had to be returned to its hangar at a cost of US$ 100,000. The woodpecker had pecked more than 75 holes in the fuel tank's insulating foam. Plastic owls are among the measures now taken to avoid repetition of the problem.

Experiment box recovered from swamps in French Guiana, near launch site of Ariane 5

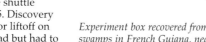

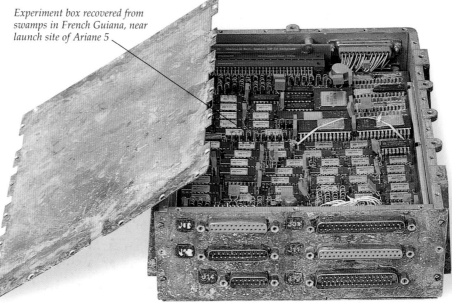

LOST PROPERTY

The failure of Mars-96 was a serious setback for the exploration of Mars and the Russian space programme. The probe had been scheduled to land four probes on Mars in September 1997. The loss of experiments on this probe came only five months after the destruction of experiments carried on the European Space Agency (ESA)'s Ariane 5, which blew up soon after launch as a result of a computer software problem.

A city in the sky is
not a modern idea.
The city of Laputa, in
"Gulliver's Travels"
by Jonathan Swift
(1727), moves up and
down from the ground
by magnetism. This
larger version of an
airborn city appears
on a 1929 comic cover.

Space stations

ABOUT 354 KM (220 MILES) ABOVE THE EARTH, astronauts are
constructing the International Space Station (ISS). When
completed it will be the largest and most complex space station
ever built. It is the tenth station in space. The first was the
Russian Salyut 1, put in orbit in 1971. Six more Salyuts
followed. America's station Skylab was used in the mid-70s.
The most successful was Mir, Russia's eighth station. Astronauts stayed on Mir
for months at a time. They carried out experiments, made observations and
collected valuable data on how humans cope with long
spells in space. The records for most hours
and longest unbroken stay by one
person in space were made on Mir.

*First Mir module
into space, crew
lived here*

*Solar panels on Soyuz
for generating
electricity*

*Soyuz craft for
ferrying crew*

*Mir docking port with
room for five visiting
craft at the same time*

MIR – A SUCCESSFUL STATION

Mir was constructed in space between 1986 and 1996. New models were
added to the original living module piece by piece. This model shows
how it looked in 1988. A photo at bottom right shows Mir in 1995 before
the final module was added. Astronauts lived on Mir for all but a short
time from February 1987 to June 2000. There were usually two or three
crew on board, but it could take six. They came from more than a dozen
countries, arriving by Soyuz craft or shuttle orbiter. Mir was brought
out of orbit and broke up in the Earth's atmosphere
in March 2001.

*Artsebarski stayed on Mir
for 145 days, Krikalyev
(right) for 310 days*

FIRST STEPS TO SPACE

Three astronauts walk across the
Baikonur launch site towards their
Soyuz TM-12 rocket to take them
to Mir in May 1991. Helen Sharman
(left), both the first Briton to go into
space and the first woman on Mir;
stayed on board for eight days. The
commander, Anatoli Artsebarski,
was flying for the first time. But
flight engineer Sergei Krikalyev
(right) was familiar with Mir as
he stayed there two years earlier.

*Spacesuits are fireproof,
waterproof, airtight,
and ventilated. The
helmet goes on last*

THE HIGH LIFE

The seventh and final Salyut space station was launched in April 1982. Salyut 7 was in orbit, about 322 km (200 miles) above Earth, until February 1991. The first crew were Anatoly Berezovoi (top) and Valentin Lebedev who spent 211 days in space, setting a record. It was also home to the first male-female crew in space.

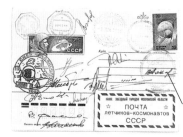

POSTCARD FROM SPACE

Cards like this one have been through a post office that was truly out of this world – the one on board Mir. The office's unique postmark was stamped by hand. The crew aboard Mir in late 1987 stamped and signed about 1,000 envelopes for stamp collectors around the world.

Sergei Avdeev stayed on Mir from September 1995 to February 1996

Signed by each astronaut on board Mir

INSIDE MIR

The inside of Mir was similar in shape and size to the inside of a train carriage. There was no floor or ceiling, so in every direction you looked there was equipment for the operation of the space station, for experiments, or for the astronauts' day to day needs.

Kvant, the first expansion module added to Mir, July 1987, was for science and astronomy

Progress docked at aft port

Progress, an unmanned craft ferried cargoes of fuel, food, water, mail, and equipment to Mir

SPACE UNION

In June 1995, the American space shuttle orbiter docked with Russian Mir for the first time. Together they were the largest craft then made in orbit. The crew aboard the American craft Atlantis had their own celebration – they were the 100th American human space launch.

Photograph of Atlantis moving away from Mir taken by Solovyev and Budarin who temporarily left Mir in their Soyuz spacecraft

HITCHING A RIDE

Anatoly Solovyev and Nikolai Budarin were taken to Mir aboard Atlantis. Once the orbiter had docked with Mir, the hatches on each side were opened. Solovyev and Budarin and the five American astronauts passed through to Mir for a welcoming ceremony. Five days later, Atlantis, carrying the Americans, left Mir, leaving the other two astronauts behind.

FOND FAREWELL

Atlantis and Mir were docked together for about 100 hours as they orbited Earth in June 1995. On board were the seven astronauts that had arrived on Atlantis, and three other astronauts who were already on board Mir. These three prepared for re-entry into gravity after more than three months in space. They returned to Earth aboard Atlantis along with medical samples they had taken while in space.

Science without gravity

Badge for
Spacelab 2 – 1985

ASTRONAUTS MONITOR, control, and perform experiments inside and outside their craft as they orbit Earth. The experiments are provided by space agencies, industry, universities, and by schools. They may be concerned with finding out how living things, like astronauts, insects, and plants, cope in space. They also cover areas such as chemical processes and the behaviour of materials. The knowledge acquired is used for planning the space future or is applied to life on Earth. Experiments may be only a part of a crew's workload or the whole reason for a space mission.

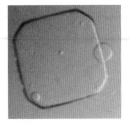

CRYSTAL
This is a space-grown human body plasma protein crystal. Crystals grown in space are larger and better ordered than those grown on Earth. Studying them provides knowledge needed to produce medicines for the human body.

Bondar checks on oat seedlings in an experiment box aboard Discovery

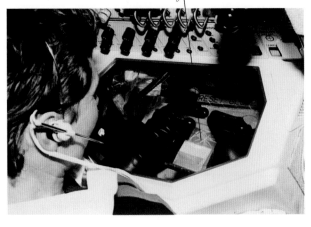

SPACELAB
A laboratory designed for space, Spacelab, flies in the payload bay of the space shuttle. It is made up of a pressurized cabin where astronauts work. In addition, U-shaped pallets outside the cabin hold instruments for direct exposure to space. It first flew in 1983. An average flight lasts ten days. Here the ESA laboratory is being fitted into the shuttle's payload bay before a flight.

GROWING FOOD
A self-contained plant growth unit was used in March 1982 to test how weightlessness affects plants. These two sets of seedlings were grown from seeds in the unit aboard Columbia. They grew to look much the same as seedlings growing on Earth, although a few small roots grew upwards.

BOXING CLEVER
Canadian Roberta Bondar was one of seven astronauts performing experiments during an eight-day shuttle flight in January 1992. Their research included studying the effects of weightlessness on lentil and oat seedlings, and shrimp and fruitfly eggs.

Oat seedlings

Mung bean seedlings

BABY BOOM
The first Earth creature to be born in space emerged from its shell on 22 March 1990. The quail chick was the result of an experiment aboard Mir. Forty-eight Japanese quails' eggs had been flown to the space station and placed inside a special incubator with ventilation, feeding, heating, waste, and storage systems attached. Then astronauts on Mir and scientists on Earth waited. On the 17th day, the first eggs began to crack open and six chicks broke free, one after the other. The birth made little impact beyond the world of space biologists; but it marked a key moment in research into reproduction in space, which will be used to plan the space future.

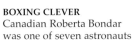

Quail's egg with crack as it begins to hatch

Chick's feathers appear as egg breaks

WORKING TOGETHER – THE EXPERIMENT
An astronaut performs experiments in space on behalf of an Earth-based scientist. Above, a scientist (right) instructs the astronaut who is going to be in charge of his telescope in space. They are checking the controls for pointing the telescope to the correct part of the Sun.

Instruments, including CHASE, mounted on Challenger equipment platform

CHASE – THE INSTRUMENT
The second Spacelab mission, which flew aboard Challenger in summer 1985, included the scientist's telescope in the orbiter payload bay. The telescope, called Coronal Helium Abundance Spacelab Experiment (CHASE), measured how much helium there is in the outer layers of the Sun.

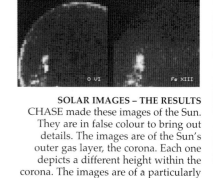

SOLAR IMAGES – THE RESULTS
CHASE made these images of the Sun. They are in false colour to bring out details. The images are of the Sun's outer gas layer, the corona. Each one depicts a different height within the corona. The images are of a particularly active part of the corona and reveal the structure of the Sun's magnetic field.

ALL IN A DAY'S WORK
The French astronaut Jean-Jacques Favier works on an experiment while wearing the Torso Rotation Experiment, which is one of a series of experiments used to study the effects of weightlessness on the human body. Favier and other crew members in the Life and Microgravity Spacelab aboard Columbia in 1996 were also tested for bone tissue loss, muscle performance, and energy expenditure.

CANDLE FLAMES
It is known that factors such as gravity and airflow influence the spread of an Earth fire, but what might affect a space fire? Tests have shown that space flames form a sphere rather than the pointed shape they have on Earth (left). They also lean strongly when subjected to an electric field (right), which leaves Earth flames unaffected.

Richard Linnehan, an American, tests his muscle response with the handgrip equipment

Astronauts use footgrips to keep themselves steady as they work

Torso Rotation Experiment

Arabella in the web she built on board Skylab

ARABELLA THE SPIDER
One space science experiment was designed by a school student from Massachusetts, USA. It involved two spiders, Anita and Arabella. The student wanted to find out how well they could make webs in weightless conditions. Their first attempts at web spinning were not perfect, but once space-adapted, they built strong and well-organized webs.

Chick squeezes out of broken egg

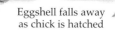
Eggshell falls away as chick is hatched

Quail chick stands up

Testing equipment

Aɴʏ ᴇǫᴜɪᴘᴍᴇɴᴛ ꜱᴇɴᴛ into space undergoes rigorous and lengthy tests long before it goes near the launch site. The process of building and testing for space starts years ahead of liftoff. Prototypes of each element of a space probe or satellite are individually built and thoroughly tested before moving on to produce the actual flight parts. About a year before launch, the parts are brought together for assembly. The whole craft is then put through another test cycle to ensure it is fully spaceworthy. It must be able to withstand the stress of launch and the environment once in space. The tests are therefore carried out in conditions as close as possible to those encountered in space.

TESTING SPACECRAFT
At their Netherlands space centre, the European Space Agency (ESA) monitor and analyze the behaviour of space probes and satellites to assess how spaceworthy the craft are. Something as simple as a speck of dust can cause a very costly short circuit later on, so the tests are carried out in controlled, clean conditions.

Exterior of the LSS, shown in detail below

Facilities for testing small- and medium-sized equipment

HUMAN TESTS
American John Bull tested a newly designed Apollo spacesuit for mobility in 1968. Bull later withdrew from training because of ill health and never made it into space. Men and women travelling into space also go through test procedures to make sure they are in good condition and will survive their trip.

ADAPTING TO SPACE
With more, and longer, space flights planned, astronauts are increasingly being tested for endurance and adaptability. They undergo tests before, during, and after flight. Tests are carried out on other humans for comparison. Volunteers are strapped down, wired up, and swung about to simulate the return from space to gravity.

Auxiliary chamber houses mirror

Light reflection from sun simulator is directed to main chamber

Chambers have temperature-controlled stainless steel shrouds

Mirror is made up of 121 pieces

LARGE SPACE SIMULATOR
The environmental conditions a craft will encounter in space are simulated by special test equipment. The European Space Agency (ESA) has been using the Large Space Simulator (LSS) since 1986 to test its space probes and satellites. It works by recreating the vacuum, heat, and solar radiation conditions of space. The craft to be tested is sealed in the main chamber, which is depressurized to achieve a vacuum. The impact of the Sun is produced by lamps, with a large mirror directing the solar beam to the craft. This is a model of the LSS that allows you to see inside.

GAS GUN
Spacecraft need to be protected from miniscule particles of space dust which can produce surface holes and craters when they collide with the craft. Scientists in Canterbury, Britain, use a gas gun to assess the damage such particles can cause. This research has provided valuable information for the design of spacecraft bumper shields.

Test using thin metal | Test using thick metal

BUMPER SHIELD
Scientists have tested different thicknesses of metal to find a way of minimizing the damage dust particles can do to space probes. A double layer bumper shield can also help reduce damage. The first layer of metal breaks up the particle and spreads out the energy.

SOLAR PANELS
The contrast of these two solar panels shows the effects of space. The piece on the right has not been used, while the piece on the left has been retrieved from space. The dents and pits caused by the impact of space particles can clearly be seen. Scientists can use this evidence to determine the size and speed of the particles.

Satellite in main chamber

Main chamber is 15 m (49 ft) high with a removable lid for easy loading

Lamp house contains 19 xenon lamps like this one

Five-metre (16 ft 5 in) door incorporating man-sized door for side access to main chamber

ENVISAT
Users of the LSS can have tests in any combination and sequence. Here the satellite Envisat is being lowered into the main chamber at the start of its final stage of tests. Once testing is completed, a craft is accepted for flight.

Sun simulator provides a uniform and stable beam

Lonely explorers

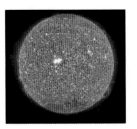

VOYAGER 1
Two Voyager craft toured Jupiter, Saturn, Uranus, and Neptune.

ROBOTIC SPACECRAFT EXPLORE SPACE for us. About the size of family cars, they are launched from Earth by rocket or space shuttle to travel to a predetermined target. On board these space probes are scientific experiments to carry out investigations, a power supply, small thruster rockets for path adjustment, and means for recording and sending data back to Earth. A probe may fly by its target, or orbit it, or land on it. Some carry a second smaller probe or lander craft for release into an atmosphere, or for touchdown on a planetary or lunar surface. Probes have investigated all Solar System planets except Pluto, taken a close look at many of the moons, comets, asteroids, and have studied the Sun.

SOAKING UP THE SUN
The Solar and Heliospheric Observatory (SOHO), the most comprehensive spacecraft to study the Sun, started its work in April 1996. Twelve different instruments on board the SOHO space probe are observing the Sun constantly.

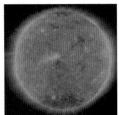

SUNNY OUTLOOK
In visible light the Sun appears calm, but SOHO is recording plenty of vigorous activity. Every day, SOHO pictures the whole Sun at four ultraviolet wavelengths (shown here), which correspond to different temperatures in the Sun's atmosphere. SOHO was designed to operate until 1998, but its life was prolonged to 2003.

Circles represent hydrogen atoms emitting radiation at a particular wavelength

Sketch of Pioneer, drawn to scale, with people to show size of a human

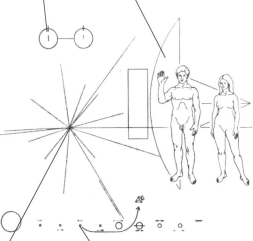

MESSAGE FROM EARTH
A few months before the launch of Pioneer 10 in 1972, it was realized that it and its sister probe, Pioneer 11, would follow paths that would eventually take them out of the Solar System. It was agreed that the probes, travelling in opposite directions, should carry messages in case any extraterrestrials come across them in the future. The messages were etched on a 15 cm (6 in) x 23 cm (9 in) gold-covered aluminium plaque.

Boom with magnetometer to measure magnetic field in interplanetary space and near Jupiter

A means of locating the Solar System in the Milky Way

Map of Solar System showing Pioneer has come from third planet (Earth) and passed close by Jupiter

BEYOND THE BELT
Pioneer 10 left Earth on 3 March 1972 for a journey to Jupiter. It was the first probe to venture beyond the asteroid belt. It took six months to emerge at the far side, successfully avoiding a collision with a piece of space rock. The probe flew by Jupiter at a distance of 130,300 km (80,967 miles) before heading for the edge of the Solar System. Space probes close to the Sun can use solar panels for power to operate and communicate with Earth. For travel beyond Mars, like Pioneer 10, electric generators need to be on board.

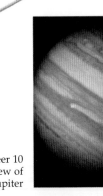

Pioneer 10 view of Jupiter

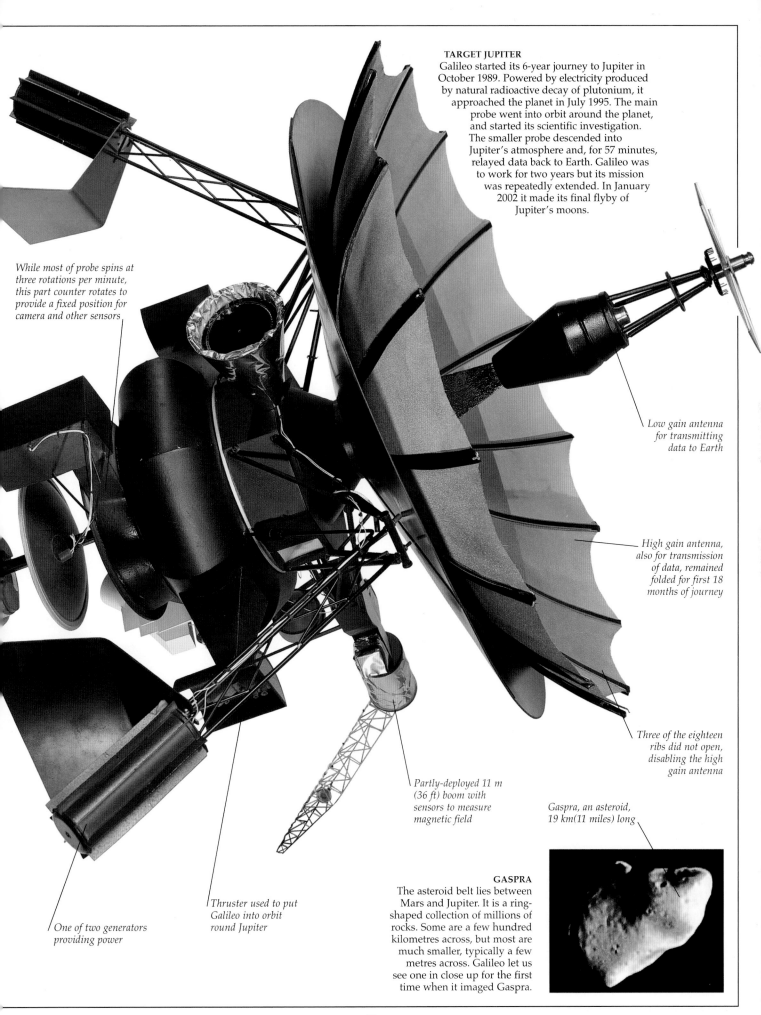

TARGET JUPITER
Galileo started its 6-year journey to Jupiter in October 1989. Powered by electricity produced by natural radioactive decay of plutonium, it approached the planet in July 1995. The main probe went into orbit around the planet, and started its scientific investigation. The smaller probe descended into Jupiter's atmosphere and, for 57 minutes, relayed data back to Earth. Galileo was to work for two years but its mission was repeatedly extended. In January 2002 it made its final flyby of Jupiter's moons.

While most of probe spins at three rotations per minute, this part counter rotates to provide a fixed position for camera and other sensors

Low gain antenna for transmitting data to Earth

High gain antenna, also for transmission of data, remained folded for first 18 months of journey

Three of the eighteen ribs did not open, disabling the high gain antenna

Partly-deployed 11 m (36 ft) boom with sensors to measure magnetic field

Gaspra, an asteroid, 19 km(11 miles) long

One of two generators providing power

Thruster used to put Galileo into orbit round Jupiter

GASPRA
The asteroid belt lies between Mars and Jupiter. It is a ring-shaped collection of millions of rocks. Some are a few hundred kilometres across, but most are much smaller, typically a few metres across. Galileo let us see one in close up for the first time when it imaged Gaspra.

In-depth investigators

On board a space probe are around 10 to 20 highly sensitive scientific instruments. These instruments of investigation record, monitor, and carry out experiments for Earth-based scientists. The information they supply enables astronomers and space scientists to build up a picture of the objects in space. The instruments are arguably the most important part of a space probe. They, however, rely on the main structure to transport, protect, and power them. Scientists often have to design instruments to work in unknown conditions and investigate objects previously viewed only from Earth. They may have to wait years before the instruments start to work and the results come in.

JOURNEY'S END
Space probes travel hundreds of millions of kilometres from Earth for years at a time. Most complete their journeys, but Mars-96, shown here, had a faulty booster rocket and failed to leave Earth orbit.

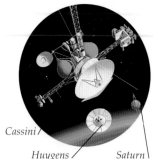

Cassini / Huygens / Saturn

SPACE PROBE TO SATURN
One of the most expensive and ambitious space probes to be built so far will reach Saturn in 2004 after a seven-year journey. Cassini will orbit the planet and its moons for four years. Huygens, a small probe, will be released to investigate the atmosphere and surface of Saturn's largest moon, Titan.

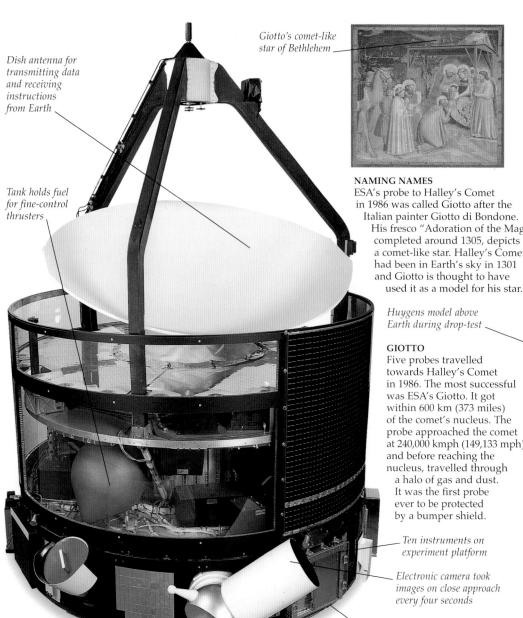

Dish antenna for transmitting data and receiving instructions from Earth

Tank holds fuel for fine-control thrusters

Giotto's comet-like star of Bethlehem

NAMING NAMES
ESA's probe to Halley's Comet in 1986 was called Giotto after the Italian painter Giotto di Bondone. His fresco "Adoration of the Magi", completed around 1305, depicts a comet-like star. Halley's Comet had been in Earth's sky in 1301 and Giotto is thought to have used it as a model for his star.

TITAN
Titan is shrouded by a thick, orange, nitrogen-rich atmosphere. Scientists do not know what to expect on Titan's surface. Huygens will land in ocean-like lakes of liquid methane or on a dry surface. Its instruments are prepared for both and will provide results in either case.

Huygens model above Earth during drop-test

GIOTTO
Five probes travelled towards Halley's Comet in 1986. The most successful was ESA's Giotto. It got within 600 km (373 miles) of the comet's nucleus. The probe approached the comet at 240,000 kmph (149,133 mph) and before reaching the nucleus, travelled through a halo of gas and dust. It was the first probe ever to be protected by a bumper shield.

Ten instruments on experiment platform

Electronic camera took images on close approach every four seconds

Bumper shield (not shown) fitted here. This side of Giotto approached comet

TESTING HUYGENS
A heat shield will protect Huygens as it drops through Titan's upper atmosphere. This will be ejected, and the instruments will test the lower atmosphere while parachutes ensure a slow descent to Titan's surface. A full-size Huygens model was drop-tested to ensure everything works in sequence.

HOW COLD?
This instrument on board Huygens will measure the temperature of gases as the probe descends through Titan's atmosphere, and liquids as it lands on its surface. The instrument will also measure how easily the gases and liquids transmit heat.

Gas or liquid flows through holes

DENSITY
If the Huygen's probe lands in liquid on Titan's surface, the level at which this instrument floats will indicate the liquid's density. It will tell us whether it is water- or treacle-like.

FIRST TOUCH
This is the part of Huygens which is expected to hit the surface of Titan first. It can measure how quickly the probe stops, and whether it has hit land or ocean. If it is land, it can tell the difference between rock, soil, and ice. If it is ocean, another instrument (left) will measure the density of the liquid.

Cable transfers data for storage then transmission

Transmitter receives and sends "beeps"

COMPOSITION CRACKER
These two pieces of Huygens equipment, speakers and receivers combined, measure how fast a "beep" sound travels from one to the other. The results help determine the density, temperature, and composition of Titan's atmosphere and surface.

Temperature and density instruments inside

Composition cracker

TOP HAT SCIENCE
The five experiments featured here were fitted together in this one piece of equipment known as the Surface Science Package (SSP). It is about the size and shape of a top hat. The SSP and five more experiments were all thoroughly tested before being fitted onto Huygens about a year before launch. International teams of scientists worked on the experiments. The SSP was prepared by a team from Canterbury, Britain.

Surface Science Package

Ocean deep

First touch

Composition cracker

This part will touch Titan first

DESCENT TO TITAN
In this artist's impression, Huygens is falling through Titan's atmosphere. It will transmit data for around two and a half hours as it falls and when it lands.

STAY COOL
Space technicians work on Huygens at facilities in Bordeaux, France. They are fitting the heat shield for protecting Huygens against high temperatures. Huygens will be submitted to temperatures about 1,800 °C (3,272 °F) to 2,000 °C (3,632 °F), but its internal temperature must not exceed 180 °C (356 °F).

OCEAN DEEP
The system of sonar is used by ships in Earth's ocean. This Huygens instrument will be the first to use the technique in space. If Huygens lands in ocean, it will transmit sound which will reflect off the ocean bed. The time taken for it to come back will give the ocean depth.

Landers and discoverers

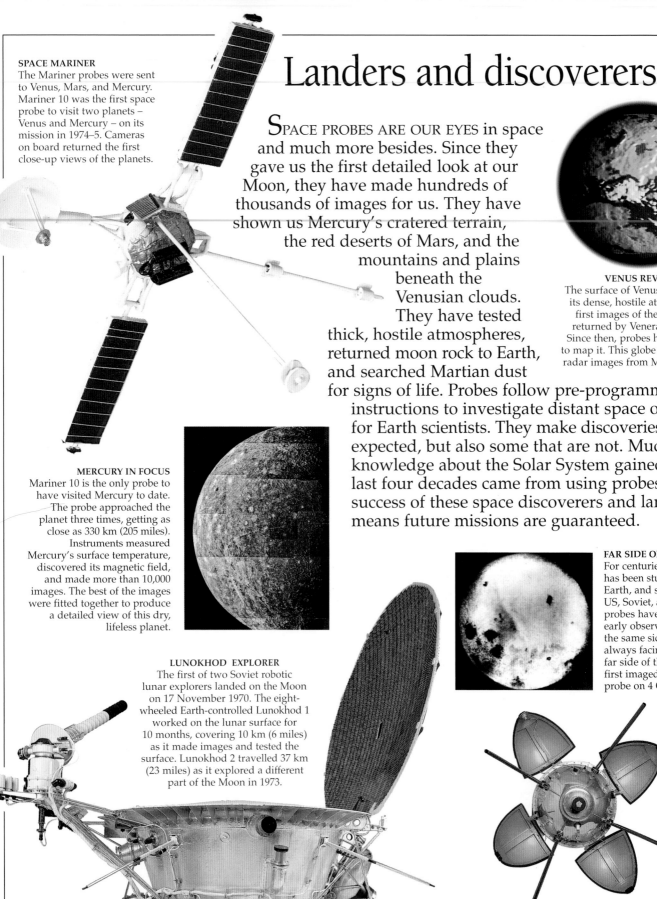

SPACE PROBES ARE OUR EYES in space and much more besides. Since they gave us the first detailed look at our Moon, they have made hundreds of thousands of images for us. They have shown us Mercury's cratered terrain, the red deserts of Mars, and the mountains and plains beneath the Venusian clouds. They have tested thick, hostile atmospheres, returned moon rock to Earth, and searched Martian dust for signs of life. Probes follow pre-programmed instructions to investigate distant space objects for Earth scientists. They make discoveries that are expected, but also some that are not. Much of our knowledge about the Solar System gained in the last four decades came from using probes, and the success of these space discoverers and landers means future missions are guaranteed.

SPACE MARINER
The Mariner probes were sent to Venus, Mars, and Mercury. Mariner 10 was the first space probe to visit two planets – Venus and Mercury – on its mission in 1974–5. Cameras on board returned the first close-up views of the planets.

VENUS REVEALED
The surface of Venus is obscured by its dense, hostile atmosphere. The first images of the surface were returned by Venera craft in 1975. Since then, probes have used radar to map it. This globe was made using radar images from Magellan in 1992.

MERCURY IN FOCUS
Mariner 10 is the only probe to have visited Mercury to date. The probe approached the planet three times, getting as close as 330 km (205 miles). Instruments measured Mercury's surface temperature, discovered its magnetic field, and made more than 10,000 images. The best of the images were fitted together to produce a detailed view of this dry, lifeless planet.

LUNOKHOD EXPLORER
The first of two Soviet robotic lunar explorers landed on the Moon on 17 November 1970. The eight-wheeled Earth-controlled Lunokhod 1 worked on the lunar surface for 10 months, covering 10 km (6 miles) as it made images and tested the surface. Lunokhod 2 travelled 37 km (23 miles) as it explored a different part of the Moon in 1973.

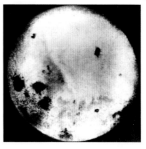

FAR SIDE OF THE MOON
For centuries, the Moon has been studied from Earth, and since 1959, US, Soviet, and Japanese probes have visited it. The early observations were of the same side, the one always facing Earth. The far side of the Moon was first imaged by a Soviet probe on 4 October 1959.

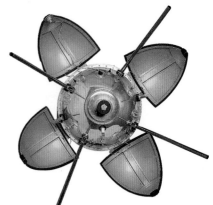

MOON DETECTIVES
The Soviet Luna series of space probes studied the Moon for almost 20 years. They were the first probes to travel to the Moon, to image the far side, to crash-land, and to orbit it. Luna 9 successfully achieved the first soft landing on 3 February 1966, and made the first panoramic pictures of the lunar surface which showed details only 1 mm across.

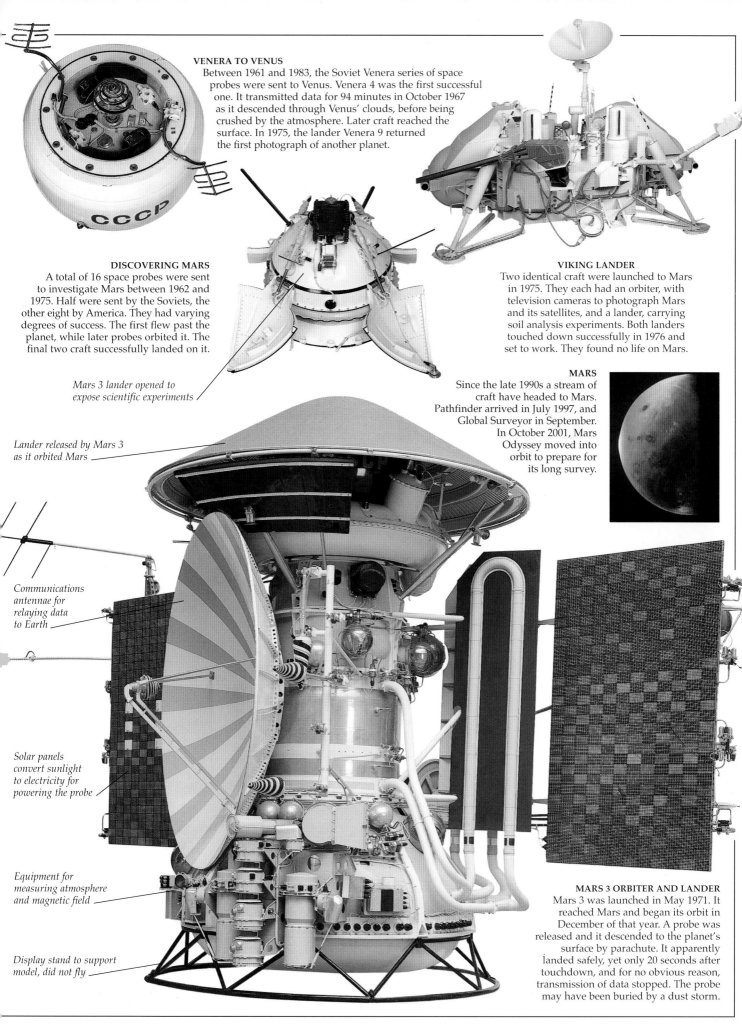

VENERA TO VENUS

Between 1961 and 1983, the Soviet Venera series of space probes were sent to Venus. Venera 4 was the first successful one. It transmitted data for 94 minutes in October 1967 as it descended through Venus' clouds, before being crushed by the atmosphere. Later craft reached the surface. In 1975, the lander Venera 9 returned the first photograph of another planet.

DISCOVERING MARS

A total of 16 space probes were sent to investigate Mars between 1962 and 1975. Half were sent by the Soviets, the other eight by America. They had varying degrees of success. The first flew past the planet, while later probes orbited it. The final two craft successfully landed on it.

Mars 3 lander opened to expose scientific experiments

Lander released by Mars 3 as it orbited Mars

Communications antennae for relaying data to Earth

Solar panels convert sunlight to electricity for powering the probe

Equipment for measuring atmosphere and magnetic field

Display stand to support model, did not fly

VIKING LANDER

Two identical craft were launched to Mars in 1975. They each had an orbiter, with television cameras to photograph Mars and its satellites, and a lander, carrying soil analysis experiments. Both landers touched down successfully in 1976 and set to work. They found no life on Mars.

MARS

Since the late 1990s a stream of craft have headed to Mars. Pathfinder arrived in July 1997, and Global Surveyor in September. In October 2001, Mars Odyssey moved into orbit to prepare for its long survey.

MARS 3 ORBITER AND LANDER

Mars 3 was launched in May 1971. It reached Mars and began its orbit in December of that year. A probe was released and it descended to the planet's surface by parachute. It apparently landed safely, yet only 20 seconds after touchdown, and for no obvious reason, transmission of data stopped. The probe may have been buried by a dust storm.

Crowded space

THE MOON IS EARTH'S ONLY NATURAL SATELLITE and its closest neighbour in space. In between is the virtual vacuum of space itself. But anyone visiting Earth for the first time might think that the volume of space immediately around Earth is crowded. Within a few thousand kilometres of its surface, there are about 1,000 operational satellites. Each one is a specialized scientific instrument following its own path around Earth. The satellites work for us in a variety of ways. Arguably, the most important are the telecommunication satellites that affect most of our lives. They give us global communication at the touch of a button, beam television pictures to our living rooms, and are used in all types of business, day and night.

TELSTAR

The first transatlantic live television pictures were transmitted in July 1962 by Telstar, a round, 90 cm (35 in) wide satellite covered in solar cells. In the years that followed, live television became an increasing part of life. By 1987, Roman Catholics on five continents could join Pope John Paul II in a live broadcast using 23 satellites.

Pocket-sized navigation systems can pinpoint your position to within 15 m (49 ft)

NAVIGATION

Aircraft pilots, yachtsmen, soldiers, and now hikers navigate their way about Earth using satellites. The Global Positioning System (GPS) uses a set of 24 satellites in orbit around Earth. The user sends a signal from a hand set, like this one, which is received by up to 12 of the satellites. By return, he learns his location, direction, and speed.

Terrorist at Munich Olympic Games

Live Aid concert finale

GOOD NEWS, BAD NEWS

Satellites can turn once local events into global occasions. In 1964, Tokyo's opening ceremony of the Olympic Games was transmitted by satellite around the world. However by 1972, at the Munich Olympic Games, terrorists had learnt that live pictures could draw attention to their cause. In 1985, satellite television broadcast Live Aid to 2 billion people worldwide.

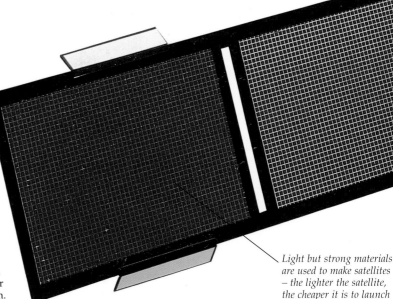

Light but strong materials are used to make satellites – the lighter the satellite, the cheaper it is to launch

BUSY LINES

A telecommunications satellite has to handle tens of thousands of phone calls at once. From the 1980s, calls across Europe have used the European Communications Satellite (ECS). ECS 1 was the first of four such satellites launched to provide 24 European countries with telephone services, television, and business links. Other areas of the world developed and used their own systems. But global schemes now exist. A series of satellites work together as they circle the world in a system known as a constellation.

GROUND CONTROL

Most satellites are launched by rocket, but some are taken into space in the payload bay of a space shuttle. Once the satellite has separated from the launcher, an on-board motor propels it into its correct orbit. Smaller manoeuvres are made by the satellite's propulsion system throughout its lifetime to maintain its correct position and attitude in space. The rocket launch centre now hands over to the satellite control centre. They use ground stations, like this one in Belgium, to track the satellite, receive its signals, monitor its health, and send commands.

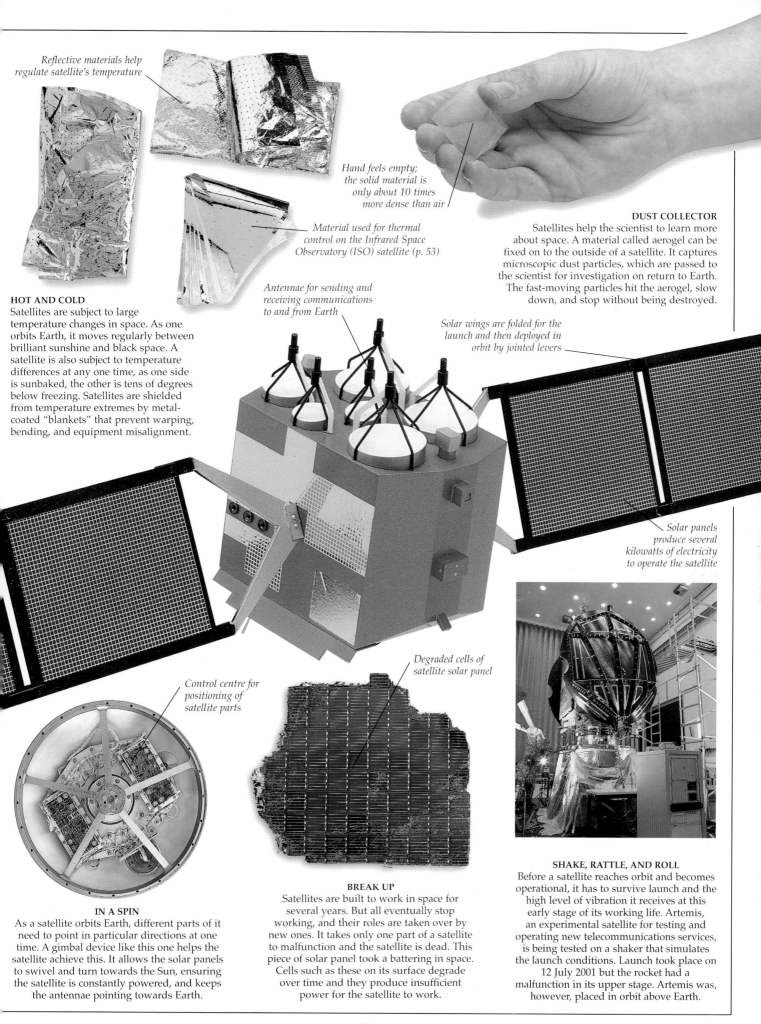

Reflective materials help regulate satellite's temperature

Hand feels empty; the solid material is only about 10 times more dense than air

Material used for thermal control on the Infrared Space Observatory (ISO) satellite (p. 53)

DUST COLLECTOR
Satellites help the scientist to learn more about space. A material called aerogel can be fixed on to the outside of a satellite. It captures microscopic dust particles, which are passed to the scientist for investigation on return to Earth. The fast-moving particles hit the aerogel, slow down, and stop without being destroyed.

HOT AND COLD
Satellites are subject to large temperature changes in space. As one orbits Earth, it moves regularly between brilliant sunshine and black space. A satellite is also subject to temperature differences at any one time, as one side is sunbaked, the other is tens of degrees below freezing. Satellites are shielded from temperature extremes by metal-coated "blankets" that prevent warping, bending, and equipment misalignment.

Antennae for sending and receiving communications to and from Earth

Solar wings are folded for the launch and then deployed in orbit by jointed levers

Solar panels produce several kilowatts of electricity to operate the satellite

Control centre for positioning of satellite parts

Degraded cells of satellite solar panel

IN A SPIN
As a satellite orbits Earth, different parts of it need to point in particular directions at one time. A gimbal device like this one helps the satellite achieve this. It allows the solar panels to swivel and turn towards the Sun, ensuring the satellite is constantly powered, and keeps the antennae pointing towards Earth.

BREAK UP
Satellites are built to work in space for several years. But all eventually stop working, and their roles are taken over by new ones. It takes only one part of a satellite to malfunction and the satellite is dead. This piece of solar panel took a battering in space. Cells such as these on its surface degrade over time and they produce insufficient power for the satellite to work.

SHAKE, RATTLE, AND ROLL
Before a satellite reaches orbit and becomes operational, it has to survive launch and the high level of vibration it receives at this early stage of its working life. Artemis, an experimental satellite for testing and operating new telecommunications services, is being tested on a shaker that simulates the launch conditions. Launch took place on 12 July 2001 but the rocket had a malfunction in its upper stage. Artemis was, however, placed in orbit above Earth.

Looking at Earth

Satellites are taking a close look at our planet. In their different orbits about Earth they can survey the whole globe repeatedly or remain over one spot. Each one concentrates on collecting a specific type of information. Weather satellites look at clouds and study the Earth's atmosphere, or record the planet's range of surface temperatures. Both man-made structures and natural resources such as water, soil and minerals, and flora and fauna, are mapped by others. Ocean currents, ice floes, and animals and birds are followed. By taking time-lapse images of Earth, satellites are making records of short- and long-term planetary changes. The data they collect can be used to predict changes, and to avoid problems like soil erosion and floods.

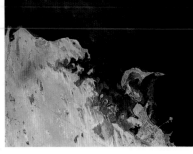

MAN-MADE DISASTER
The Landsat 5 satellite gives a bird's eye view of a vast oil slick on the Saudi Arabian shore line in 1991. False colours have been added to the image. The slick is coloured rusty red. The oil had been deliberately released one month earlier by Iraqi soldiers in Kuwait.

Paris

FOUR CORNERS
The European Remote Sensing (ERS) series of satellites started work in 1991. ERS-1 returned several thousand pages worth of information every second. ERS-1 made these four views of parts of Europe (above and in other corners) in 1992. Its successor ERS-2 was launched in 1995, and charts the world's ozone layer every three days.

City of Detroit

Small, harmless transmitter is attached to neck collar

BIRD SPOTTING
The fish-eating Steller's sea eagle breeds in far eastern Russia. As winter approaches, the sea starts to freeze and the eagle's supply of food is cut off. Satellite tracking follows the birds as they fly south to spend the winter on the Japanese island of Hokkaido.

DEERSTALKER
Small transmitters are attached to animals, like this red deer. As the deer moves about, a signal is released which is picked up by satellite. Over time, its habitual movements are revealed. By knowing where animals breed, feed, and spend winter, conservationists can protect such sites and so conserve the creatures.

Geometrically shaped man-made fields stand out

EYE IN THE SKY
The French Earth observation satellite, Spot-1, was launched in 1986. Every 26 days, it photographed the whole of Earth's surface. On board were two telescopes, each observing a 60 km (37 mile) wide strip of land below the satellite. Objects only 10 m (33 ft) across were recorded. This Spot-1 picture of farmland in Canada was made in July 1988. False colours identify different crops at different stages of growth. Lake St Clair is at the top and Lake Erie at the bottom of the picture, both shown in blue.

London

MAN ON THE MOVE

Air-, sea-, and land-based forces all use satellite systems. Their planes and ships are installed with equipment using navigation systems. For the single soldier in remote terrain, such as desert, a navigation backpack is the answer. It will tell him where he is and in which direction to move. A portable communications system keeps him in touch with other troops.

Portable folding satellite dish

Vienna

Solar cells supply energy for Meteosat to function

Upper platform carries communication equipment

WEATHER WATCH

Meteosat satellites have been in operation since 1977. Weather satellites such as Meteosat are in geostationary orbit, which means they orbit in the same time Earth turns, so they stay above a particular spot on Earth and monitor the same region. Data from these and other satellites are combined to study global weather patterns, and used to make daily forecasts.

ERUPTION

Images of natural phenomena, such as volcanoes, are made by satellites and by astronaut-operated equipment on board their craft. Smoke and ash from an active volcano can be monitored, and aircraft warned away. Ground movements of a few centimetres to several metres, that may warn of a volcanic eruption, can be detected and the alarm raised.

LOOK AND LEARN

Events and places on Earth can be watched by people thousands of kilometres away because of communication satellites. People can learn about different nations and cultures from their own homes. In 1975, over 2,400 villages in India were given satellite dishes and televisions. Direct broadcasting by satellite instructed them on hygiene and health, family planning, and farming methods.

Zeeland, the Netherlands

Looking into space

Scientific satellites are used by astronomers to look away from the Earth and into space. They are telescopes that collect and record data in much the same way that telescopes do on Earth. But from their vantage point, they can study the Universe 24 hours a day, 365 days a year. Space telescopes operate in a range of wavelengths. Much of the information they collect, such as that at X-ray wavelengths, would be stopped from reaching ground-based instruments by Earth's atmosphere. Data collected by telescopes working in optical, X-ray, infrared, ultraviolet, microwave, and other wavelengths are combined to make a more complete view of space. This data is collected, stored, and sent to a ground station, where it is decoded by computers. Astronomers all over the world have been looking at the Universe in this way for about 30 years.

EARLY ASTRONOMY
Astronomers once recorded their findings in drawings, like this one. Today, electronic devices record data transmitted from telescopes in Earth orbit.

Plane of Milky Way

MIRROR IMAGES
Tremendous amounts of energy are needed to create X-rays, so wherever they are detected, there is violent activity. The Chandra X-ray Observatory has been imaging and studying X-ray sources since August 1999. It was launched aboard the Columbia shuttle orbiter in July 1999. Chandra works in high Earth orbit: it travels a third of the way to the Moon and orbits Earth once every 64 hours 18 minutes.

OUR GALACTIC CENTRE
The High Energy Astrophysics Observatory X-ray satellite telescope took this false-colour X-ray view of our Galaxy. The view covers two-thirds of Earth's sky. The plane of the Milky Way crosses the centre of the picture from left to right. The black, then red, areas are the most intense X-ray emitters. The yellow and green areas emit less, and the blue, the least X-ray energy.

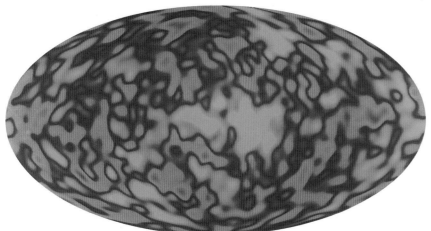

RIPPLES IN THE SKY
In 1992, the COsmic Background Explorer (COBE) satellite discovered slight temperature differences in the Universe's microwave background radiation. In this false-colour microwave map of the whole sky, the average temperature of the background radiation is shown as deep blue. The pink and red areas are warmer, and the pale blue cooler. These were the ripples scientists predicted should exist in background radiation created by the Big Bang.

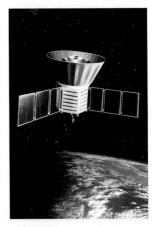

MICROWAVE IMAGES
The first satellite telescope to look at space in the microwave region was launched by rocket into an orbit about 917 km (570 miles) above Earth. COBE started work in late 1989. It provided the first observational proof for the theory that the Universe was created in a huge explosion we call the Big Bang about 13 billion years ago.

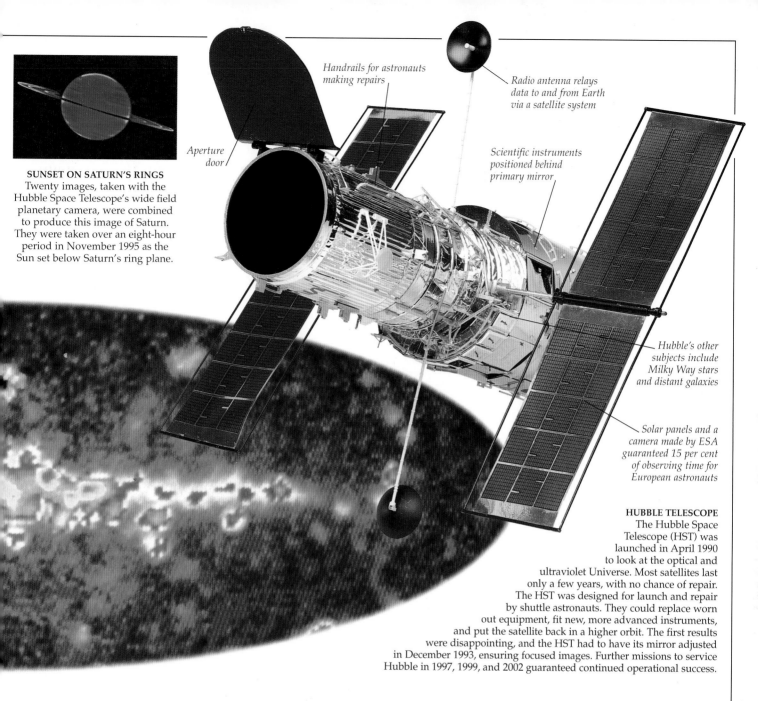

SUNSET ON SATURN'S RINGS
Twenty images, taken with the Hubble Space Telescope's wide field planetary camera, were combined to produce this image of Saturn. They were taken over an eight-hour period in November 1995 as the Sun set below Saturn's ring plane.

Handrails for astronauts making repairs

Aperture door

Radio antenna relays data to and from Earth via a satellite system

Scientific instruments positioned behind primary mirror

Hubble's other subjects include Milky Way stars and distant galaxies

Solar panels and a camera made by ESA guaranteed 15 per cent of observing time for European astronauts

HUBBLE TELESCOPE
The Hubble Space Telescope (HST) was launched in April 1990 to look at the optical and ultraviolet Universe. Most satellites last only a few years, with no chance of repair. The HST was designed for launch and repair by shuttle astronauts. They could replace worn out equipment, fit new, more advanced instruments, and put the satellite back in a higher orbit. The first results were disappointing, and the HST had to have its mirror adjusted in December 1993, ensuring focused images. Further missions to service Hubble in 1997, 1999, and 2002 guaranteed continued operational success.

ISO being tested by ESA, before launch in 1995

Launch of ISO by Ariane 4, November 1995

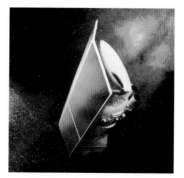

Impression of ISO in orbit

Picture taken by ISO of supernova, an exploding star

INFRARED OBSERVATIONS
The European Space Agency's Infrared Space Observatory (ISO) made 26,000 scientific observations in its working lifetime, from 1995 to 1998. From its elliptical orbit, which took it from 1,000 km (621 miles) to 70,000 km (43,497 miles) above the Earth, ISO used its 60 cm (2 ft) mirror to observe the near and distant Universe, making on average 45 observations a day. Data on materials in Saturn, the birth of stars, colliding galaxies, and water ice in our Galaxy were all sent to ESA's tracking station in Madrid.

The future in space

SPACE TRAVEL IS GOING to be as familiar in the years ahead as air travel became in the 20th century. It will involve men, women, and children travelling more often, and making longer trips. People will once again be on the Moon's surface and the first astronauts will walk on Mars. Travellers will have the choice of going as a tourist for a short stay in a hotel, or in the more distant future setting up home in a Moon or Mars base. Astronauts will continue to explore and work from space stations. They will be joined by a new breed of robotic space workers operating telescopes and mining equipment on the Moon. These ideas are being considered or planned by space agencies and businesses in America, Europe, Japan, and China right now.

Satellite dish

Command module

Space shuttle

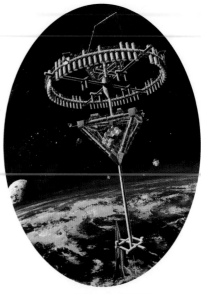

HOLIDAY RESORT
Japanese business men are planning an Earth-orbiting hotel, shown above, followed by one on the Moon. The hotel is built around a 240 m (787 ft) elevator shaft. The guest rooms are on a wheel that turns three times a minute. It will be a base for sightseeing tours to the Moon, spacewalks, and unique sports and games in weightlessness.

SPACE FOR EVERYONE
The cost of launching to space is currently very high. Space tourists need a new reusable vehicle that runs cheaply and frequently. One that could be used for straightforward space flights, for that special occasion such as a space wedding, and for docking with an orbiting hotel. From Earth spaceport to orbiting hotel would take an hour.

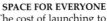

FISHY BUSINESS
New ways of providing food are needed if long duration space trips are to be a reality. At present, astronauts take their food with them, or have stocks replenished by visiting crews. Japanese crews are fond of eating fresh fish, and wish to farm fish in space to produce sushi. To this end, these non-edible medaka fish have mated and produced young in space.

SPACE PLANE
NASA is working on new re-usable space planes to replace the American space shuttle. They have built and flown test vehicles (without crew) which, like the shuttle, take off vertically and glide to a landing. The new craft are to be safer, more reliable, and less expensive, and to be used for both government and commercial needs.

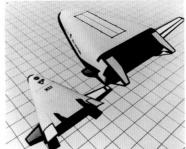

SPACE PLAY
The space scientists, engineers, and astronauts of the near future are children today. These cardboard toys came free with McDonalds Happy Meals in the US in 1991, and were free McDonalds give aways in Germany in 1993. They were produced in collaboration with The Young Astronaut Council who encourage children in America to study science, maths, and space.

Lunar rover

ROBOT TRAVELLER
Unmanned craft will continue to be used to explore our space neighbourhood. Space probes will fly by, and orbit, the planets and their moons. Landers will return with Martian and asteroid rock, and dusty snow from the heart of a comet. Robots will work on space stations. Those at Moon or Mars bases will be designed to operate on lunar and planetary surfaces.

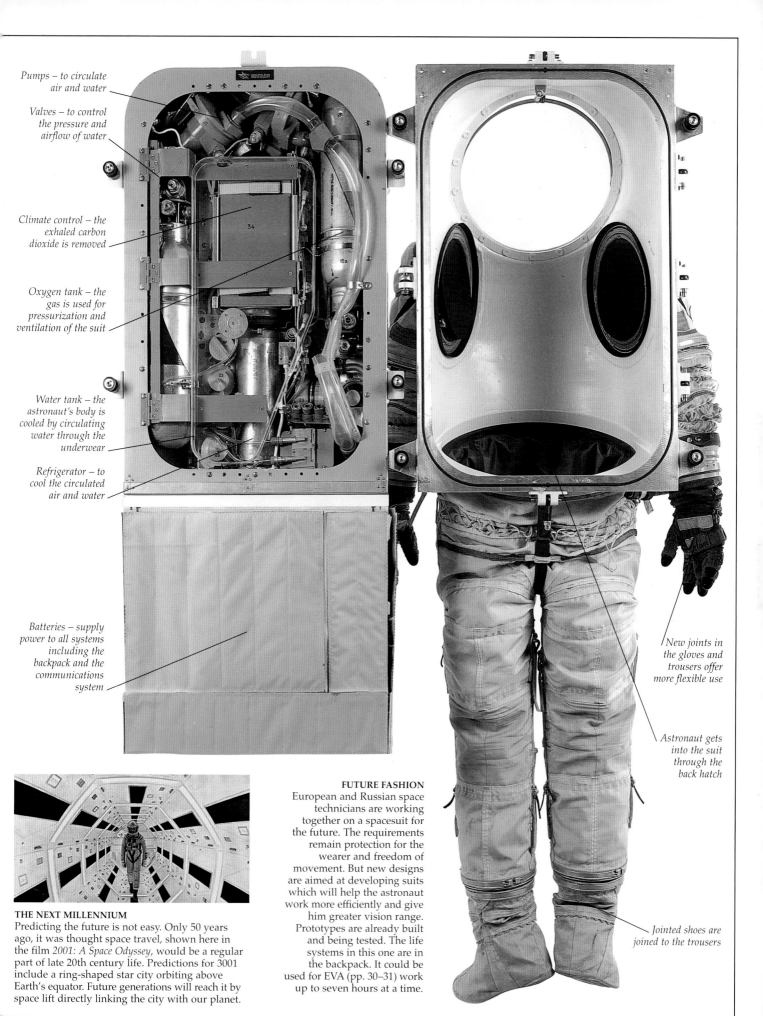

Pumps – to circulate air and water

Valves – to control the pressure and airflow of water

Climate control – the exhaled carbon dioxide is removed

Oxygen tank – the gas is used for pressurization and ventilation of the suit

Water tank – the astronaut's body is cooled by circulating water through the underwear

Refrigerator – to cool the circulated air and water

Batteries – supply power to all systems including the backpack and the communications system

New joints in the gloves and trousers offer more flexible use

Astronaut gets into the suit through the back hatch

Jointed shoes are joined to the trousers

THE NEXT MILLENNIUM
Predicting the future is not easy. Only 50 years ago, it was thought space travel, shown here in the film *2001: A Space Odyssey*, would be a regular part of late 20th century life. Predictions for 3001 include a ring-shaped star city orbiting above Earth's equator. Future generations will reach it by space lift directly linking the city with our planet.

FUTURE FASHION
European and Russian space technicians are working together on a spacesuit for the future. The requirements remain protection for the wearer and freedom of movement. But new designs are aimed at developing suits which will help the astronaut work more efficiently and give him greater vision range. Prototypes are already built and being tested. The life systems in this one are in the backpack. It could be used for EVA (pp. 30–31) work up to seven hours at a time.

Spin-offs

SPACE INDUSTRY RESEARCH is used to benefit our everyday lives. Technologies and techniques designed for use in space have been transferred or adapted for life on Earth, often in fields totally unrelated to the original research. An everyday item such as food wrapping was developed from reflective film used on satellites. Car control systems used by one-handed drivers came from the one-handed technique used in the Lunar Rover, and modern smoke detection systems use technology developed for smoke detection on the Skylab space station. Tens of thousands of spin-offs have come from space research, many of them have been adapted for medical use.

LASER BEAM
Robot and laser technology developed for space is used in equipment for people with disabilities. The boy above, who is unable to speak, is wearing a headpiece with laser equipment. By using the laser beam to operate a voice synthesizer, he is able to communicate.

INSULIN PUMP
Robert Fischell, an American space scientist, invented an insulin pump for diabetics. Once implanted in the body, the device automatically delivers precise pre-programmed amounts of insulin. The pumping mechanism is based on technology used by the Viking craft that landed on the planet Mars.

KEEPING CLEAN
An industrial cleaning method which is quick, easy to use, and harmless to the environment has grown out of space research. Rice-like pellets of dry ice (solid carbon dioxide) are blasted at supersonic speeds to remove surface dirt. On impact the ice turns to gas, the dirt falls away, and the underlying material is unharmed.

Mercury astronauts

THE SPACE "LOOK"
The first US astronauts, on the Mercury rockets, wore silver suits designed to reflect heat. The space look was transferred to haute couture when French fashion designer André Courrèges produced his "space age" collection in 1964. Within months, off-the-peg space-influenced fashions were available to everyone.

Silver kidskin outfit including cap with visor

Artificial hand and control system

HAND CONTROL
The micro-miniaturization of parts for space has been adapted for use on Earth. Artificial limbs with controls as small as coins have been developed. This makes the limbs lighter and easier to use. Devices that are no larger than a pinhead and can be placed in a human heart to monitor its rhythm are another space technology spin-off.

SPACE ON THE PISTE
Protective clothing designed for astronauts is now used on the ski slopes. The Apollo helmet design, which gave the astronauts fog-free sight, has been adapted for use in ski goggles. Electrically heated or fan-controlled goggles prevent moisture condensing inside, and the goggles from fogging up.

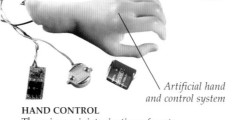

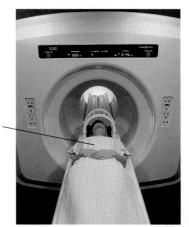

Patient enters body scanner to have body imaged

SHARP VIEW
An image-enhancement technique devised to improve the sharpness of Moon photographs is used in medical photography. It gives doctors a better basis for diagnosis by providing more accurate images. Body scanners give a much clearer overall view of what is happening inside the human body.

BAR CODE SCANNING
A trip to the supermarket means an encounter with space technology – from the food you buy to the scanner that reads bar codes to register the prices. Many of the ready-to-eat and dried meals introduced in the 1980s and 1990s are the result of space research.

BRACE YOURSELF
A metal alloy of nickel and titanium called nitinol is used in teeth braces. Nitinol was originally developed for space equipment such as antennae. The antennae are compacted for launch, before being expanded to full size in space. Nitinol was the ideal material for the job as it has the ability to return to its original shape after bending. Back on Earth, nitinol allows braces to exert continuous pull on teeth. This reduces the number of brace changes needed as the teeth are pulled into shape.

Nitinol arch wires held in place by coloured fittings apply pressure to straighten teeth

Image shows inside and outside of hand at the same time

Kidney dialysis machine removes waste materials from the patient's blood

False colour is added to make features stand out

HUMAN HAND MAP
Techniques developed to enhance satellite images of the Earth have been used to make maps of the human body for medical purposes. In this computer image of a hand with fingers extended, the contour of each finger shows the shape of the hand. At the same time, the structure of the bones underneath is revealed.

Digital display

HELPING HAND FOR HOSPITALS
Many of the results of space research are found in hospitals around the world. For example, reflective blankets used to retain an accident victim's body heat, kidney dialysis machines for purifying blood, special beds for burns patients, and miniaturized television cameras worn on a surgeon's head to allow others to watch and learn from an operation, have all been developed from space technology.

TIME UNDER PRESSURE
Space spin-offs are everywhere in daily life. Watches have digital displays, and glass capable of surviving increased gravitational force. Clothes are made with lightweight, thermal fabrics, qualities essential for space materials. Athletic footwear has stay-dry insoles, and sports helmets and shin guards are lined with shock-absorbing foam.

Working together

At the dawn of the space age, in the late 1950s, only a handful of countries were working to get into space. Just two, the USA and the Soviet Union, had the money and the know-how to succeed, and they worked in isolation to outdo each other. Today, things are different. Tens of countries are involved in the space industry. They pool knowledge and resources to build space probes and launch satellites. The old rivals, America and Russia, have joined with others to build the International Space Station (ISS).

FIRST CREW
On 2 November 2000, the first crew to live on the ISS moved in. They were Yuri Gidzenko, William Shepherd and Sergei Krikalev (left to right). They arrived on a Soyuz craft but left by space shuttle 138 days later. The three are from America and Russia, but crew from Italy, Canada, France and Japan have also stayed on the ISS.

CONSTRUCTING THE INTERNATIONAL SPACE STATION
The ISS is being assembled in space. Construction started in December 1998 and will take about eight years. Over 100 parts, delivered in up to 50 launches, are fixed together by astronauts aided by cranes, tools and a robotic arm. The ISS came alive when James Newman (below) and Jerry Ross connected and powered up the first two modules, Zarya and Unity.

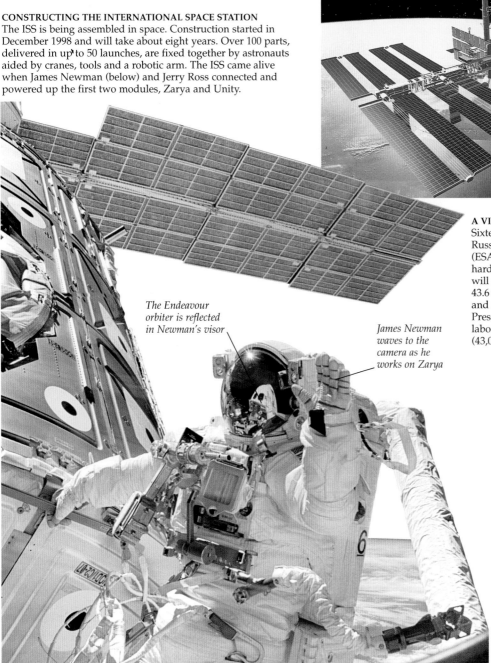

The Endeavour orbiter is reflected in Newman's visor

James Newman waves to the camera as he works on Zarya

A VISION OF THE ISS COMPLETED
Sixteen countries are working on the ISS: the US, Russia, Canada, Japan, 11 European Space Agency (ESA) countries and Brazil. Each contributes hardware and expertise. On completion, the ISS will measure 108.5 m (356 ft) by 88.4 m (290 ft) by 43.6 m (143 ft). Up to seven astronauts will live and work there for three to six months at a time. Pressurised living modules are connected to six laboratories and work stations, and 4,000 sq metres (43,000 sq ft) of solar panels provide the power.

Unity

ZARYA AND UNITY
Russian-built Zarya was the first piece of the ISS to go into space. Zarya arrived in November 1998. It is a control-module and provided power through the early assembly stages. Unity, the US-built connecting-module arrived in December, and the two were joined. This view was taken in June 1999 by a shuttle crew who fastened tools and cranes to the outside, and delivered equipment.

Zarya

CHINA IN SPACE

China has a fast-developing space industry. One of its objectives is to have more ties with other space nations. Its Long March rockets have already launched satellites for foreign customers. No one knows whether its Shen Zhou programme of manned launches will lead to international collaboration of manned flight. A monkey, a dog, a rabbit and some snails were launched and returned safely in January 2001. The launch of Chinese astronauts – taikonauts – will make China only the third nation to launch humans.

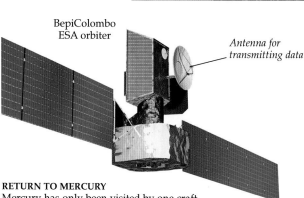

MARS EXPRESS

The European Space Agency's Mars Express starts its six-month journey to Mars in June 2003. Ground stations in Australia and French Guiana will keep it on course. On arrival it will release its lander, Beagle 2. Mars Express will spend the next two years in orbit round the planet. Its seven instruments will monitor Mars, and its antenna will transmit data between it, Earth and Beagle 2.

Artist's impression of Mars Express in orbit around Mars after the release of Beagle 2

LANDER BEAGLE 2

The mini-probe, Beagle 2, is a British project benefiting from technical and scientific support from a further 12 countries. Once jettisoned by Mars Express, it will head for the surface of Mars to look for chemical traces of life, past or present, in the rocks, the soil and the atmosphere.

BepiColombo ESA orbiter

Antenna for transmitting data

RETURN TO MERCURY

Mercury has only been visited by one craft, Mariner 10 back in 1974 and 1975. Now two spacecraft are being prepared for investigative missions to the planet. The American Messenger will orbit for one year from late 2009, and the European Space Agency- (ESA-) led BepiColombo (above) will explore Mercury and its environment on arrival in 2012. BepiColombo has three separate elements. Two, an orbiter and a lander, are being provided by ESA. The third part, another orbiter, is Japanese. This orbiter will observe Mercury's magnetic field and its interactions with the solar wind.

Four conical booster rockets

The liquid oxygen and kerosene fuel of the rocket's boosters and lower first stage provide the thrust to get the rocket off the ground

IN A CLUSTER

Most European Space Agency (ESA) countries and the US provided hardware for the Cluster satellites (above) built to investigate Sun–Earth interactions. Here they are undergoing pre-launch tests in Munich, Germany. ESA consists of 15 countries and has a head office in France, specialist centres in The Netherlands, Germany and Italy, a launch base in French Guiana and ground stations worldwide.

SPACE LAUNCHER

A European–Russian company uses Soyuz-Fregat rockets to launch space probes and satellites from the Baikonur Cosmodrome in Kazakhstan. The Soyuz rocket has a 98% success record and is one of the most reliable launchers in the world. A Soyuz-Fregat launched two of the Cluster satellites on 16 July 2000 (left). The remaining two flew on 9 August 2000. The Soyuz-Fregat carrying Cluster was a three-stage rocket. Mars Express will also use this type of rocket. Its launcher will have an additional fourth stage to put Mars Express onto its interplanetary flight path.

21st century exploration

SPACE EXPLORATION has helped us learn an enormous amount about the Universe around us. The learning continues as the 21st century unfolds. Robotic probes are returning to worlds already seen at first hand, and investigating others for the first time. New techniques will enable craft to travel faster and journey farther. New satellites replace those that have served us well. While some continue to give us a global perspective of our home planet, others look into deep space and reveal even more of the Universe.

EARLY SUCCESS

The NEAR space probe was one of the first successes of the 21st century. NEAR (Near Earth Asteroid Rendezvous) left for the asteroid belt in 1996. It reached its target, the asteroid Eros, and on 14 February 2000 began to orbit it. On 12 February 2001, scientists changed NEAR's flight plan and landed the probe on the asteroid – another first.

COST CUTTER

Some late-1990s space probes were designed to be faster and cheaper than earlier probes and still bring better results. The success of two such probes, Pathfinder to Mars and NEAR to Eros, has meant this approach continues in the 21st century. StarDust (right), launched in 1999, is keeping its cost down by taking seven years to complete a round-trip to Comet Wild-2. In January 2006, it will return to Earth with the first particles collected from any comet.

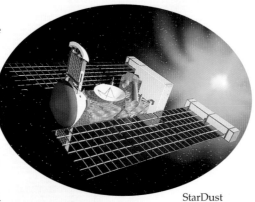

StarDust

TESTING TIME

New technologies are constantly being developed for use in spacecraft. They undergo long and extensive testing before use. A failure in space could mean the end of an otherwise successful mission. NASA's New Millennium programme is designed to speed up space exploration by testing advanced technologies in space itself. The probe Deep Space 1 tested 12 new technologies during its three-year mission to asteroid Braille and Comet Borelly. It tested a new form of engine (the ion propulsion engine), a miniature camera and computer software that let a craft think and act on its own.

Cassini just after the release of Huygens

Antenna for transmitting data collected by Cassini and Huygens

Huygens

Deep Space 1 being launched by Delta rocket in October 1998

PLANETARY PROBES

Cassini is the first major planetary probe of the 21st century. It is also one of the largest and most complex ever built. It was launched in October 1997 and flew by Jupiter in December 2000 en route to its target, Saturn. On arrival, it will release the mini-probe Huygens (p. 44-45). Cassini is the fourth mission to Saturn. It was visited last by Voyager 2 in 1981. Other planetary probes are in preparation for Mercury, and for the first time, one will travel to distant Pluto, the only Solar System planet not visited so far.

EYE ON SPACE

New, more powerful and sophisticated telescope satellites are working, or are being prepared for work, in space. The European Space Agency's XMM-Newton (XMM stands for X-ray Multi Mirror) was launched in December 1999. It is the most powerful X-ray telescope used in orbit and the largest science satellite ever built in Europe.

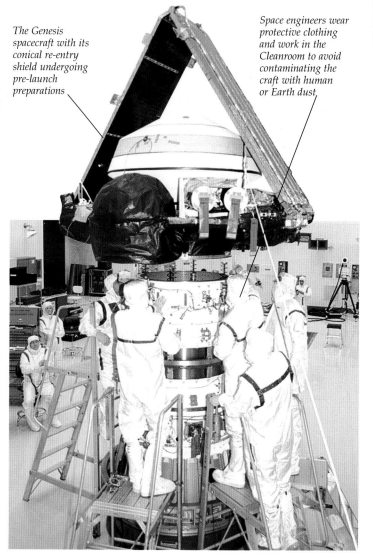

The Genesis spacecraft with its conical re-entry shield undergoing pre-launch preparations

Space engineers wear protective clothing and work in the Cleanroom to avoid contaminating the craft with human or Earth dust

EYE ON EARTH

Envisat is the largest and most advanced Earth observation satellite ever built in Europe. It is the size of an articulated truck and orbits Earth 14 times a day. Its has ten instruments that monitor our planet and can detect natural or man-made changes on land, in water or in the air. In its 10-year lifetime, it will send one million PCs-worth of information back to the European Space Agency's ground station in Sweden.

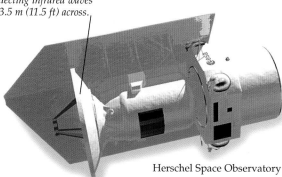

SAILCRAFT

Scientists are investigating forms of propulsion that could take craft to the edge of the Solar System and on, towards the stars. One approach is to sail across space without the need of an engine, or fuel. The craft in this artwork, known as the sailcraft, has wafer-thin sails. The accumulative pressure of sunlight on the sails would propel the craft on its journey.

Artist's impression of the sailcraft

The main mirror for collecting infrared waves is 3.5 m (11.5 ft) across.

Herschel Space Observatory

NEW GENERATION

The Herschel Space Observatory (above) is one of a group of science satellites being prepared for work in the 21st century. It is the European Space Agency's new-generation infrared telescope. Once launched in 2007, it will observe at wavelengths not covered before. Unusually, it will be in orbit 1,500,000 km (932,000 miles) from Earth. The Next Generation Space Telescope, the replacement for the Hubble Space Telescope, is due for launch in 2009.

SAMPLE RETURN

Robotic space probes travel to different parts of the Solar System and investigate them on site. But scientists sometimes need to investigate material from other worlds themselves. The Genesis mission, launched on 8 August 2001, is collecting material from the Sun for return to Earth. After orbiting the Sun for two years, Genesis will return with solar wind particles – material flowing out from the Sun. Scientists will compare the composition of these particles with that of the planets to learn more about the way the Sun and the planets formed from a cloud of gas and dust some 4,600 million years ago.

Did you know?

Victory for solar car Nuna

Space technology can be used to improve designs on Earth. In 2001, a Dutch solar car, called Nuna, developed using European space technology, won the World Solar Challenge. Nuna completed the 3,010-km (1,870-mile) race across Australia in just 32 hours and 39 minutes.

On 31 July 1999, eminent geologist Gene Shoemaker became the first person to be "buried" on the Moon. His ashes were aboard Lunar Prospector when it was launched on 6 January 1998. The craft circled the Moon for 18 months and then crash landed onto the surface.

Experiment to test the effects of weightlessness

In the future, it is hoped to send astronauts on longer missions farther into space. To prepare for this, scientists are investigating the long-term effects on the human body of living without gravity. One experiment involved getting volunteers to lie at an angle of 6° (a position that simulates many of the effects of weightlessness) non-stop for three months.

A shuttle orbiter uses 2,600–3,000 m (8,500–10,000 ft) of runway from touchdown to wheel stop, compared to around 900–1,200 m (3,000–4,000 ft) used by a commercial airliner.

About five minutes before touchdown, a shuttle orbiter makes two sonic booms. The first is generated by the nose, and is followed rapidly by the second, generated by the wings.

The drag chute slows down the space shuttle orbiter as it lands.

By 2000, the reusable shuttle fleet had notched up a total of 100 flights since the shuttle program began in 1981. It has carried over 600 passengers and spent a total of 2.5 years in space. Each orbiter is designed for 100 flights so there are plenty more trips to come.

NASA is still in contact with Pioneer 10, the probe that was launched for Jupiter in 1972. In mid-2001, the probe was 11.7 billion km (7.3 billion miles) away from Earth and travelling at 35,800 kph (22,200 mph).

When the Pathfinder probe landed on Mars in 1997, it was inside a giant ball of airbags for protection. The probe bounced 15 times on the surface, then rolled to a stop and the airbags deflated. The three panels of the probe then opened to expose the instruments and to allow the Sojourner Rover to take off down the ramp and explore the surface of Mars.

Up to half of all astronauts vomit during their first few days in space, so a good supply of "barf" bags is vital.

In the weightlessness of space, dust does not settle but constantly floats around. ISS astronauts sneeze around 100 times a day.

The European Space Agency held a competition to name the four Cluster satellites that were launched in 2000 to study the interaction between the Sun and the Earth's magnetic field. The winner chose the names of four dances – Tango, Salsa, Samba and Rumba – because the satellites would be "dancing" in formation in space.

The Hubble Space Telescope cannot afford to suffer from camera-shake. Its incredible instruments can lock onto a subject and hold still, deviating less than the width that a human hair would appear from 1.6 km (1 mile) away.

In 1966, Eugene Cernan, from Gemini IX, did a spacewalk of two hours seven minutes, beating the previous record of 36 minutes. During this time, the craft had orbited Earth so Cernan has the honour of being the first man to walk around the world. This was a tough task in itself, but Cernan then had trouble getting into the craft and closing the hatch. When he took off his suit, he emptied almost a litre (1¾ pints) of sweat from his boots.

The Martian landscape

The solar panels of Pathfinder

Ramp

Sojourner Rover next to rock nicknamed Yogi

Deflated airbag

The explosion of Challenger, 1986

Q Why did the Challenger space shuttle explode in 1986?

A The day of the Challenger launch was exceptionally cold for Florida, and the low temperature affected the seal on one of the sections of the solid rocket boosters. Fuel began to escape and, 73 seconds after launch, the fuel caught fire and exploded. The space shuttle program was suspended for two years after the tragedy for all aspects of safety to be reviewed.

Q What sort of temperatures occur in space? Is it hot or cold?

A The temperature on Earth ranges from –70 to 55 °C (–94 to 131 °F), but in space, temperatures range between –101 to 121 °C (–150 to 250 °F). The temperature depends on whether you are in sunlight or in shadow.

Q Are there any plans to send a probe to Pluto? How long would it take to get there?

A Yes, space scientists are working on a mission called New Horizons. The launch is planned for 2006, and the probe will "flyby" Pluto and its moon Charon 10 years later. It will then continue into the Kuiper Belt – a ring of icy objects that lie beyond Neptune's orbit. The probe will not take the direct route but will go past Jupiter, using the planet's gravity to hurl it into the far reaches of the Solar System.

Q When will people other than astronauts be able to travel in space?

A They already can – if they have a lot of money. In April 2001, Californian millionaire Dennis Tito became the first space tourist when he paid around £14 million for an eight-day trip to the International Space Station. Tito enjoyed the experience and said, "I was worried that I might not feel good in space. I turned out to feel the best I've felt in my entire life."

Q Is life in space almost completely silent? Is it quiet in a spacecraft, too?

A Astronauts experience extremes of noise and silence. Space is silent because there is no air through which sound can travel. On an EVA (extra vehicular activity), astronauts cannot hear each other, even if they are side by side. They communicate by radio. But air is pumped inside a spacecraft, and life inside is very noisy. A launch is louder still – a hundred million times louder than a normal conversation!

Pieces of Mir blaze through the Earth's atmosphere

Q What happened when the space station Mir was abandoned?

A On 23 March 2001, after 86,320 orbits, Russian Mission Control fired engines to knock Mir out of orbit and into the Earth's atmosphere, where it broke up. This could be seen from Earth, as the picture above, taken from Fiji in the South Pacific, shows. Some pieces burned up in the atmosphere, but larger parts landed in the Pacific Ocean between Chile and New Zealand.

Space tourist Dennis Tito

Record Breakers

LONGEST SINGLE STAY IN SPACE
On 22 March 1995, Russian cosmonaut Valeri Poliakov returned to Earth after 438 days 17 hours 58 minutes and 16 seconds in space. Poliakov also holds the overall endurance record of 679 days in two missions.

LONGEST EXTRA VEHICULAR ACTIVITY
On 11 March 2001, US astronauts Susan Helms and Jim Voss spent 8 hours 56 minutes working outside on the ISS.

OLDEST SPACE TRAVELLER
On 29 October 1998, US astronaut John Glenn became the oldest space traveller ever at the age of 77. This was not Glenn's first space record. Thirty-six years earlier, on 20 February 1962, Glenn became the first American to orbit the Earth in the Mercury Friendship 7 spacecraft.

MOST PEOPLE IN SPACE AT ONE TIME
On 14 March 1995, there were 13 astronauts in space simultaneously: seven astronauts were aboard the space shuttle Endeavour, three were in Mir, and three were in Soyuz.

Timeline

EVER SINCE SPUTNIK went into orbit in 1957, the story of space exploration has advanced at a fast and furious pace. Below is a timeline of some of the most significant achievements. Today, we rely on satellites overhead and we take it for granted that astronauts work on a space station and that probes travel to other worlds. All this was once a dream. Who knows what the rest of the 21st century will bring.

Sputnik's outer shell protected a radio transmitter and batteries

Sputnik 1

4 OCTOBER 1957
Sputnik 1, the world's first artificial satellite is put into Earth orbit by the Soviet Union. The Space Age has begun.

Space dog, Laika, aboard Sputnik 2

3 NOVEMBER 1957
The first living creature, a Soviet dog called Laika, travels into space on Sputnik 2.

2 JANUARY 1959
Soviet probe Luna 1 becomes the first craft to leave Earth's gravity.

13 SEPTEMBER 1959
Luna 2 is the first craft to land on another world when it crash lands on the Moon.

10 OCTOBER 1959
Soviet Luna 3 spacecraft returns the first pictures of the Moon's far side.

12 APRIL 1961
Soviet cosmonaut Yuri Gagarin becomes the first person to travel in space.

5 MAY 1961
Alan Shepard travelling in Freedom 7 is the first American in space.

Yuri Gagarin

10 JULY 1962
Telstar 1, the first realtime communications satellite, is launched by the USA.

16 JUNE 1963
The first woman, Soviet cosmonaut Valentina Tereshkova, travels into space.

18 MARCH 1965
Soviet cosmonaut Alexei Leonov makes the first spacewalk (EVA). He is secured to Voskhod 2 by a tether.

15 JULY 1965
US probe Mariner 4 completes the first successful Mars flyby.

3 FEBRUARY 1966
Soviet craft Luna 9 becomes the first to land successfully on the Moon.

24 DECEMBER 1968
American craft Apollo 8 is the first manned craft to leave Earth's gravity and orbit the Moon.

20 JULY 1969
The first humans walk on another world. American astronaut Neil Armstrong is the first to walk on the Moon, Buzz Aldrin the second.

20 SEPTEMBER 1970
Soviet probe Luna 16 lands on the Moon. It will be the first craft to collect soil and return it to Earth.

17 NOVEMBER 1970
The first wheeled vehicle on the Moon, Soviet Lunkhod 1, starts its work.

19 APRIL 1971
Launch of the first space station, Soviet Salyut 1.

Buzz Aldrin walks on the Moon, 1969

The reflection of photographer Neil Armstrong can be seen in Aldrin's visor

19 DECEMBER 1972
Return to Earth of Apollo 17, the sixth and last manned mission to the Moon.

3 DECEMBER 1973
US spacecraft Pioneer 10 is the first craft to flyby Jupiter after becoming the first to cross the asteroid belt.

29 MARCH 1974
US spacecraft Mariner 10 makes the first flyby of Mercury and provides the first detailed look at the planet.

17 JULY 1975
Apollo 18 astronauts and Soyuz 19 cosmonauts make the first American–Soviet space rendezvous.

22 OCTOBER 1975
Soviet craft Venera 9 transmits the first images from Venus's surface.

20 JULY 1976
The US probe Viking 1 becomes the first craft to land successfully on Mars.

1 SEPTEMBER 1979
The US probe Pioneer 11 makes the first flyby of Saturn.

12 APRIL 1981
Launch of the first reusable space vehicle, US space shuttle, Columbia.

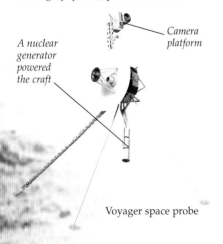

Columbia, the first shuttle in space

24 JANUARY 1986
US probe Voyager 2 arrives at Uranus, after making flybys of Jupiter and Saturn.

A nuclear generator powered the craft

Camera platform

Voyager space probe

The docking module for visiting craft. The station grew as new modules were added up until 1996

Space station Mir

20 FEBRUARY 1986
The first module of the Soviet space station, Mir, is launched into orbit.

13 MARCH 1986
The European probe, Giotto, makes the first close flyby of a comet when it approaches Halley's Comet.

24 AUGUST 1989
Voyager 2 makes the first flyby of the planet Neptune.

24 APRIL 1990
Launch of the Hubble Space Telescope on board the space shuttle Discovery.

15 SEPTEMBER 1990
US probe Magellan starts a three-year project to map Venus as it orbits the planet.

29 OCTOBER 1991
American probe Galileo makes the first flyby of an asteroid, Gaspra, before becoming the first probe to orbit Jupiter (arrived 1995).

15 OCTOBER 1997
The space probe Cassini is launched to start its journey to Saturn.

20 NOVEMBER 1998
Zarya, the first part of the International Space Station, is launched aboard a Soviet Proton rocket.

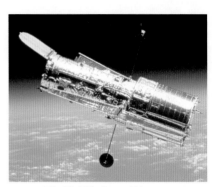

The Hubble Space Telescope

2 NOVEMBER 2000
The first crew to stay aboard the International Space Station arrive on the Soviet rocket Soyuz-TM 31.

12 FEBRUARY 2001
The probe NEAR (Near Earth Asteroid Rendezvous) becomes the first to land on an asteroid after orbiting Eros for one year.

The International Space Station (ISS), August 2001

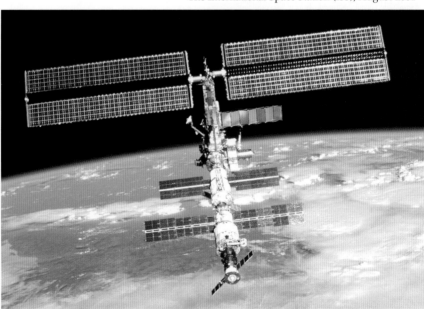

Find out more

DRAMATIC ADVANCES in space exploration have been echoed by innovative ways to learn about space. Books and TV were once the only source of information. Today, visitors to space centres all over the world are able to see where the action happens for themselves, share the experiences of an astronaut, do hands-on experiments in space science and see the craft that explore space for us. Now, via the internet, anyone can access the very latest stories and pictures of space exploration.

THE EURO SPACE CENTER, TRANSINNE
These children are doing experiments in space science at the Euro Space Center at Transinne in Belgium. The Space Center covers all aspects of space exploration, but with particular emphasis on the work of the European Space Program. Exhibits include a big display on the Columbus Laboratory, the European contribution to the International Space Station. Visitors to Transinne can also try out some of the simulators used to train astronauts (see pages 24-25).

Full scale model of the orbiter Endeavour

KENNEDY SPACE CENTER
This picture shows the Kennedy Space Center, part of the huge Kennedy Space Complex in Florida, USA, where space shuttles are launched. As well as visiting the exhibits of the Space Center (where an astronaut is available to answer questions), visitors can see the LC39 Observatorium Gantry in the Space Shuttle Launch Complex and the Launch Control Center. The public can also watch space shuttle launches at the site. A Shuttle Launch Schedule and further information about this are available from Kennedy Space Center.

MISSION CONTROL, HOUSTON, USA
Space shuttles launch from Florida, but after just two minutes control passes to the Mission Control Center (above) at NASA's Johnson Space Center, in Houston, Texas. This is the centre of the manned flight program where NASA astronauts are trained. Space Center Houston has a museum and offers a tour around the site to see the X-38 Assembly Building, the Shuttle Mock-up Facility and Mission Control. During a space shuttle mission, visitors can watch activity in the Mission Control Center from a viewing gallery.

Spacecraft hang from the ceiling of the museum in Star City

STAR CITY, MOSCOW
Exhibits telling the story of the Russian manned flight program can be seen in the museum of the Yuri Gagarin Cosmonaut Training Facility at Star City, an hour from Moscow. This purpose-built town is the home and training centre of Russian cosmonauts and the site of Russian Mission Control.

Other places to visit

NATIONAL SPACE CENTRE, LEICESTER, UK
A museum dedicated to achievements of space exploration, space science and technology.

CITE DE L'ESPACE, TOULOUSE, FRANCE
An interactive and educational space museum in the chief city of the French space industry.

NOORDWIJK SPACE EXPO, THE NETHERLANDS
A visitor centre that tells the story of space exploration past, present and future. It is next to the European Space Agency's Technical Centre

NATIONAL AIR AND SPACE MUSEUM, WASHINGTON, USA
The home of a large collection of original space hardware, including the Apollo 11 module, which returned the first men on the Moon.

EXPLORING SPACE ON THE WEB

Space is one of the most exciting subjects to explore on the internet because there is so much information available. You can, quite literally, explore space from your computer. In particular, space agencies such as NASA and the European Space Agency (ESA) have very comprehensive websites full of facts and images. Below are suggestions for a few subjects you may want to investigate further with the addresses of some useful websites.

THE EUROPEAN SPACE PROGRAM
Details of ESA projects and news stories can be found on their homepage. The ESA launch pages give details of the next launch. Interactive features take you on a tour round the ESA Spaceport in French Guiana, South America, and show a launch sequence.

- ESA homepage:
  www.esa.int
- ESA launch pages:
  www.esa.int/export/esaLA

ESA uses Ariane 5 to take payloads into space

EXPLORING SPACE
To find out more about planets in our Solar System, such as Mars (above), search on the ESA and NASA sites for details of visiting craft and future missions. For the latest images from deep space, look on the Hubble Space Telescope website.

- Space Telescope Science Institute:
  www.stsci.edu

Flags from the 15 ESA countries adorn the rocket boosters

THE SPACE SHUTTLE
Information on everything to do with the space shuttle, from the launch schedules and menus on board, to the position of the spacecraft (updated every hour), can be found on the NASA spaceflight website. It is also possible (with the right software) to watch live coverage of space missions online.

- NASA space shuttle information:
  www.spaceflight.nasa.gov/shuttle
- For watching space shuttle online:
  www.spaceflight.nasa.gov/realdata

The rocket boosters are used up and discarded within two minutes of launch

The orbiter vibrates wildly as it lifts off from the launch pad

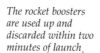

THE INTERNATIONAL SPACE STATION
For information on the International Space Station (ISS), look on the NASA spaceflight site and on the ESA ISS pages. There are also sites that will calculate when you should be able to see the ISS from wherever you are in the world.

- For information on seeing the ISS:
  www.heavens-above.com

ADDITIONAL WEBSITES

- Observatorium, NASA site for Earth and space data:
  observe.arc.nasa.gov
- British National Space Centre:
  www.bnsc.gov.uk
- Japanese Space Programme:
  www.nasda.go.jp
- Russian Space Agency:
  www.iki.rssi.ru
- Jet Propulsion Laboratory for data on space probes:
  www.jpl.nasa.gov
- Space science site for children:
  kids.msfc.nasa.gov

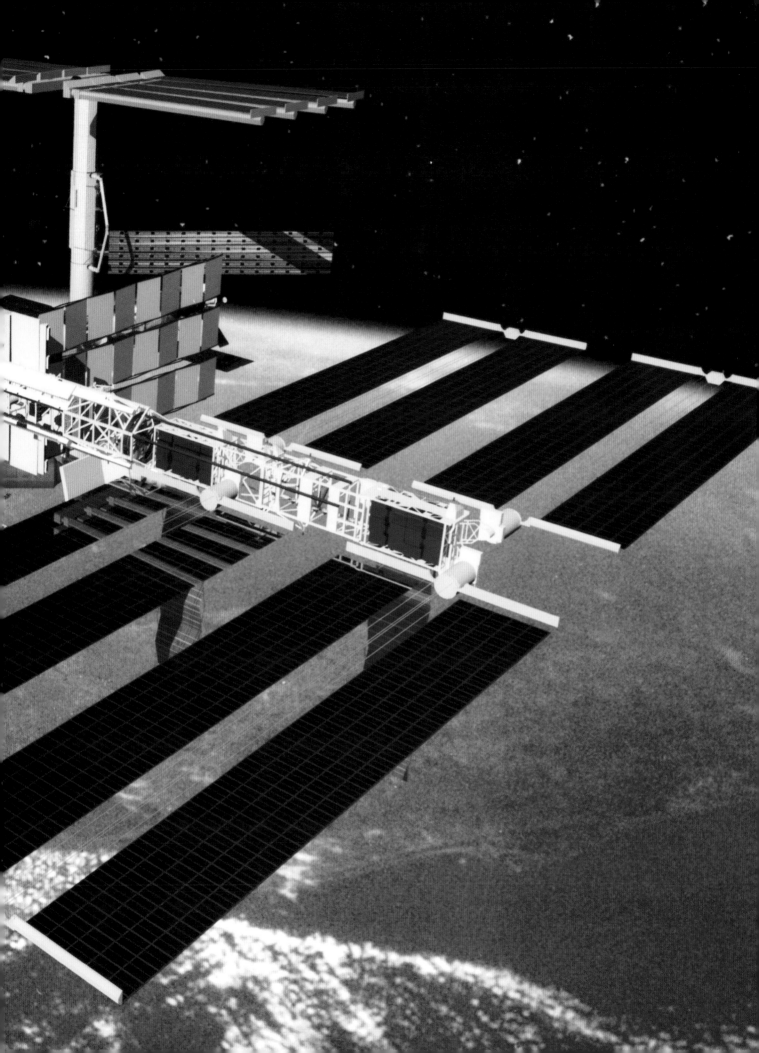

Eyewitness titles in this series:

Ancient Egypt

Ancient Greece

Ancient Rome

Bird

Castle

Crystal & Gem

Future

Medieval Life

Music

Pirate

Pyramid

Religion

Rock & Mineral

Shark

Skeleton

Viking

Volcano

Weather

Whale

Future titles to include:

Arms & Armour

Dance

Dinosaur

Early People

Explorer

Flying Machine

Fossil

Horse

Insect

Invention

Knight

Mammal

Mummy

Ocean

Plant

Pond & River

Seashore

Shipwreck

Sport

Victorians

Index

Acknowledgements

Dorling Kindersley would like to thank:
Heidi Graf and Birgit Schröder of the European Space Research and Technology Centre (ESTEC), Noordwijk, the Netherlands for their invaluable assistance; Alain Gonfalone; Hugo Marée, Philippe Ledent, Chantal Rolland, and Massimiliano Piergentili of the Euro Space Center, Transinne, Belgium (managed by CISET International) for their cooporation and patience; Helen Sharman; Neville Kidger; Dr John Zarnecki and JRC Garry of the University of Kent; MK Herbert, Ray Merchant; Dr David Hughes, Dr Hugo Alleyne, and Dr Simon Walker of The University of Sheffield; Prof John Parkinson of Sheffield Hallam University; Amalgam Modelmakers and Designers; Nicholas Booth; JJ Thompson, Orthodontic Appliances; Hideo Imammura of the Shimizu Corporation, Tokyo, Japan; Dr Martyn Gorman of the University of Aberdeen; Dr Peter Reynolds; Prof Kenichi Ijiri; Dr Thais Russomano and Simon Evetts of King's College London; Clive Simpson; Karen Jefferson and Elena Mirskaya of Dorling Kindersley, Moscow Office.

Design and editorial assistance: Darren Troughton, Carey Scott, Nicki Waine

Additional research: Sean Stancioff
Additional photography: Geoff Brightling
Photographic assistance: Sarah Ashun
Additional modelmaking: Peter Minister, Milton Scott-Baron
Endpapers: Anna Martin
Index: Chris Bernstein

Picture credits:
Dorling Kindersley would like to thank:
Moscow Museum, Science Museum and US Space and Rocket Centre Alabama,
Photographs by: Stephen Oliver close-up shot 21t; James Stevenson, Bob Gathney

The publisher would like to thank the following for their kind permission to reproduce their photographs:
t=top c=centre a=above b=below l=left r=right
Algemeen Nederlands Persbureau: 62tl. BOC Gases, Guildford 56cla. Bridgeman Art Library, London/Adoration of the Magi, cc.1305 by Giotto, Ambrogio Bondone (c.1266-1337) Scrovgeni (Arena) Chapel, Padua. Casio Electronics Co Ltd 57br. Bruce Coleman / Robert P Carr 35clb. CLRC 45c. Corbis: 69tl; Bettmann 64bl; Jim Sugar Photography 68bc, 69tl; Corbis UK 56bl/Corbis-Bettman-UPI

19cra, 21bl, 48cr. ESTEC 38cla. European Space Agency: 17bl, 30bc, 31c, 33br, 36-37, 37tr, 40tr, 41cr, 44br, 45bl, 45cb, 49c, 50tl, 50bl, 51tr, 51crb, 51br, 53bl, 53tl, 53br, 58cla, 59tr, 59cra, 59cl, 60clb, 61tl, 61br, 62cl/Alain Gonfalone 39cra. Euro Space Centre, Transinne: Euro Space Centre, Transinne 68tl. Mary Evans Picture Library 8tr, 8cl, 8tl, 9tl, 20tl, 22tl, 36tl; CSG 1995/Genesis Space Photo Library 12bl; 59tl; 61tr; Dr. Martyn Gorman, University of Aberdeen 50c / NASA 58tl, 60br, 61cl, 68cl, 68cr. Ronald Grant Archive/When Worlds Collide/Paramount 54clb, 2001: A Space Odyssey/MGM 55bl; Hasbro International Inc 9br. Hulton Getty 21tr, 21bc; Professor Kenichi Ijiri 54cla / Image Bank 57tl; Used with permission from McDonald's Corporation 54l. Matra Marconi Space UK Ltd 51tr / Mattels UK Ltd 9cb. NASA 7tr, 7br, 10clb, 11tr, 11cr, 13clb, 15tl, 16tl, 16cl, 17cla, 17br, 17tr, 20clb, 20bc, 23tr, 30tr, 30clb, 30cr, 31tr, 32br, 32tl, 33cla, 33bl, 33tr, 34cl, 34bl, 34crb, 35cla, 35tl, 37bl, 37br, 38cr, 38crb, 38clb, 38tl, 39cb, 39cl, 40cl, 52tl, 54tr, 54cb, 56tr, 56bl, 58bc, 58ca, 58tr, 58cra, 58br, 60-61, 62-63, 62b, 63tl, 63br, 64-65, 64r, 65cr, 65cl, 65br, 69tr, Finley Holiday Films 69b, Johnson Space Center 58bl / JPL 22-23, 46tr, 46c. NASDA 15cb. The National Motor Museum, London 15tc. The Natural History Museum, London 23cla. Novosti (London) 18bl, 19crb, 20crb, 34tr, 34bc, 35cb, 37tl, 46crb. Professor John Parkinson/NASA 8br, 39tl,39tc, 39tr. Popperfoto 15tr / Mark Baker/Reuters 63tr;

Mikhail Grachyev / Reuters 63bl; Popperfoto-Reuter 21crb, 21crb, 44tl. Rex Features 8bl, 9cl, 9tr, 36bc, 48cl. Science Museum/Science and Society Picture Library 15ca. Science Photo Library/Dr Jeremy Burgess 8cb/Robert Chase 57c/CNES, 1988 Distribution Spot Image 50-51cb/ Luke Dodd 10cr/EOSAT 50tr./ ESA 59cr / Victor Habbick Visions 61cr, Johns Hopkins University Applied Physics Laboratory 60tl / Will and Deni McIntyre 56tl / Larry Mulvehill 57bl/NASA 11cb, 17tl, 19bl, 34c, 44tr, 52cl, 52-53, 52br, 52bl, 59br, 59tl / NASA, 22-23b, 58cr, 60cla, 62tr, 65tc, 69cr; Novosti 14tr, 19tr, 19tl, 64cl; Starsem 59bc; David Parker 48clb/Princess Margaret Rose Orthopaedic Hospital 56cb/Roger Ressmeyer, Starlight 12br; Smith Sport Optics Inc, Idaho 56c; Shimizu Corporation 54tr/ Tony Morrison/ South American Pictures 8cr; Spar Aerospace (UK) Ltd 13tl. Tony Stone Images/Hilarie Kavanagh 51cr/ Marc Muench 11br/Charles Thatcher 56br; Dr John Szelskey 41tl, 44cra; Michael Powell/Times Newspapers Ltd 40bl; Dean and Chapter of York-York Minster Archives 9bl.
Jacket credits: NASA front main image; Popperfoto back br.

Every effort has been made to trace the copyright holders. Dorling Kindersley apologizes for any unintentional omissions and would be pleased, in such cases, to add an acknowledgement in future editions.